Did you know Warren Buffett, the world's wealthiest stock investor, is quoted as saying three books have shaped his investment philosophy? For more than half a century, he used the information provided in these three books to go from nothing – to a massive $39 billion net worth. The three books that gave him this wisdom are: *The Wealth of Nations* (pub. 1776) by Adam Smith, *Security Analysis* (pub. 1934) by Benjamin Graham, and *The Intelligent Investor* (pub. 1949), also by Benjamin Graham.

In fact, Benjamin Graham was Buffett's professor at Columbia and the most influential financial advisor he ever had.

So, have you ever tried reading Graham's books? Many might agree the books are as exciting as listening to Ben Stein read the 30th page of The Wall Street Journal.

It is time we fixed that. Instead of keeping these billion-dollar secrets hidden behind thousands of pages of financial jargon, I wrote one simple guide – *Warren Buffett's Three Favorite Books.*

If you're looking for a guide that explains how the wealthy really think and buy assets, you're in the right place. This isn't a get-rich-quick book. Instead, this is where your investing techniques take a turn in the road. This book will teach you how to accumulate assets and become very wealthy over decades of wise decisions and proper asset valuation. The best part about the book is the methods are taught in an easy-to-follow and understandable scenario for all to enjoy!

Warren Buffett's

3

Favorite Books

A guide to *The Intelligent Investor, Security Analysis,*
and *The Wealth of Nations*

Preston G. Pysh

Library of Congress Cataloging-in-Publication Data

Pysh, Preston G.
    Warren Buffett's 3 Favorite Books/Preston G. Pysh
    p. cm.
    ISBN 978-0-9829676-2-1
    1. Business & Investing. 2. Personal Finance. 3. Finance. 4. Investing.

Book Design by Pylon Publishing

ATTENTION: SCHOOLS AND BUSINESSES

Pylon Publishing books are available at quantity discounts with bulk purchase for educational, business, or sales promotional use. For information, please write to info@pylonpublishing.com.

For Demi, Kelly, Jenny, and Tyler

May we care for others the same as we care for ourselves

CONTENTS

ACKNOWLEDGMENTS

Thank you to my wife, Demi Pysh, who has stood by me every waking moment. Your strength and encouragement is far greater than anyone will ever know. Even though I sometimes talk about the most boring things on the planet, you always listen and encourage me to be myself. Kelly and Jenny thanks for tolerating my dinner table business talk, I'm sure it's every 14 and 11 year olds dream. You're the best nieces an uncle could ever have.

I especially want to thank Mac Davis for his input on the financial risk portion of the book. All of chapter 5 was written by Mac and his contributions are greatly appreciated.

I'd like to thank Jonathan Kozial for giving me the idea to write this book back in 2010. Your confidence in my ability to write such a book was the motivation I needed to get off my butt and execute. By the way, you're not as bad of a pilot as everyone says you are.

After completing the manuscript, Jacob Marceaux was the first person to willingly read my content. Your selflessness and candid input cannot be repaid. I'm so thankful for your friendship and contributions to this project.

I'd like to thank Adam Berlew for his input to the content found at www.BuffettsBooks.com, and Ruth Goodman for her tireless efforts editing the content.

I'd like to thank my parents Bill and Gwen Pysh for their continued support and feedback.

There are numerous people that have contributed to the success of this book and the content that surrounds it. Although you might not be mentioned by name, I appreciate your contributions equally. Thank you.

PART I
THE FOUNDATION

In the late 1990's, the world's wealthiest stock investor, Warren Buffett, purchased a massive sum of bonds during the country's largest growth spurt in stock market history. As dot-com investors made exuberant amounts of money, experts used Buffett's financial decisions as a punching bag for every business talk show across the country. Many cast the "Oracle of Omaha" as a "has-been" and irrelevant. As everyone knows, the five-year boom was quickly followed by an abrupt bust, leaving countless investors broke. It should come as no surprise that the billionaire investor was poised and prepped with billions in cash on hand (from his bonds) to pick up the scraps of the fallen "wannabe" traders, exponentially increasing his wealth after the crash.

Almost any investor would argue that Buffett possesses the most keen and instinctual ability to predict market behavior. I would argue the exact opposite. In fact, I'd actually declare Buffett is more reactive than proactive in his investment strategy.

Now I'm sure you might be raising an eyebrow reading that last paragraph, but as you read through this book, you'll quickly understand that Buffett's ability to simply adapt to the current market conditions, and always know the value of his investments, is what made him the best stock investor of the 21st century.

As suggested on the cover of this book, Warren Buffett has shaped his investing technique from three books. Unfortunately for many, these books are very difficult to read and understand – especially if you are just starting on your financial journey. That's why I wrote this book: to provide an abbreviated and understandable version of those important investing books.

Everyone wants the crystal ball in order to make a lot of money. The problem compounds when those same people want to make a lot of money quickly. If you're one of those people, you've got the wrong book. This book will not teach you how to pick the company that will turn your thousands into millions in under three years. If that's what you're looking for, you'll be disappointed. With that said, if you want to learn how to value stocks, exercise patience, and accumulate assets over time, then this book should be a great start for your financial journey.

You don't have to be from Wall Street to know there is an inordinate amount of money to be made in financial markets. This is something everyone feels and believes but doesn't understand how to implement. The reason most investors can't take advantage of this intuition is a few simple words: emotions, patience, and knowledge.

Let's start with the basics. People acquire financial wealth by accumulating assets. In short, an asset is anything that adds money to your pocket each month instead of taking it away. If accumulating assets is the key to building wealth, accumulating liabilities would accomplish the exact opposite. So one can quickly agree that purchasing a $60,000 vehicle that looses $15,000 a year in equity is an enormous liability.

Understanding the simple rule that asset accumulation is the means to financial success, I'll waste no time in identifying the two most lucrative ways to build assets: owning businesses and providing loans. Surprised? You shouldn't be. Businesses are nothing more than purchasing stocks, and providing loans is nothing more than purchasing bonds.

Why are these two assets more lucrative than other investments? The answer is one word: variance. Since billion-dollar businesses and loans are minced into microscopic pieces and sold at tangible prices (i.e., $20 a share), millions of traders can drastically miss-price the value of successful assets. Market behaviors then allow you to take advantage of miss-priced assets due to greed and fear.

The mistake that nearly all Americans make, to include members of Wall Street, is they don't recognize the importance and connection between both assets. At the root of the wealth equation is the firm understanding that stocks and bonds go together like a husband and wife. This is something many individuals fail to realize and take advantage of. This is something that investors like Warren Buffett and Benjamin Graham understood and capitalized on. This stock to bond relationship is the key to a billionaire's propagation and existence.

This brief introduction is an overview of the ideas you'll learn throughout this book. Instead of providing a narration of each of Buffett's three favorite books, I've instead combined all the information into a format that provides an easier method for understanding Buffett's fundamentals and beliefs. I've tried very hard to ensure the topics remain interesting and understandable so you remain motivated to learn these vital techniques. Let me add, this book isn't designed to replace The Intelligent Investor, Security Analysis, and The Wealth of Nations. Instead, this book will provide you with a starting point and general overview of the most important aspects found in those profound books.

For many, investing is almost impossible to understand and enjoy. I truly hope this book is different for you. Without further delay, enjoy reading Part I of this book. At the end of the first part, you'll develop a fundamental understanding of stocks, bonds, the market, and how they're all related.

Chapter 1
The Neighborhood Business
Stocks 101

Section 1

Twelve-year-old Billy owned a lemonade stand. The stubborn little entrepreneur refused to let his parents pay for anything. In fact, throughout the summer he had purchased all his own supplies and products from the money he made. Lucky for him, the family's house was situated along the fifth hole of the town's golf course. As an added bonus, the family's home was one of the only domiciles adjacent to the course. As the thirsty golfers reached the farthest point from the clubhouse, Billy's drinks always hit the spot. Despite his young age, Billy had strong rules and discipline. For instance, before pouring every drink he would blow into the plastic cup to clear it of any grass or debris. The customers loved that one. One of his more impressive disciplines was his inability to stop working until he made a $10 profit each day. He truly was a determined little boy.

As luck would have it, some of the hackers would occasionally ask Billy if he had any golf balls for sale. Quickly capitalizing on the potential for growth, Billy started selling golf balls in addition to his fresh cup-blown lemonade. By the middle of the summer, Billy's friends couldn't believe how much money he had made. As one might expect, Billy's good friend, Joe, was mesmerized by Billy's money and business. Unable to control himself, Joe had to talk to Billy about his business. On a Wednesday afternoon, Joe pedaled his bike down to Billy's lemonade stand on the fifth hole.

As his bike crackled like a motorcycle from the baseball cards that were attached to his spokes, Joe shouted 100 feet away, "Hey, Billy, I want to buy your business!"

Fake smiling and embarrassed, Billy continued pouring the lemonade for his chuckling customers.

One older golfer whispered under his breath, "Don't undervalue the business, Billy," as they all laughed and prepared for their tee shots.

Turning around like a spring-loaded clay pigeon launcher, Billy forcefully told Joe, "This business isn't for sale, period."

Joe, already prepared for the rejection, quickly countered with, "Fine, but I'll give you $300 for everything." Without hesitation, Joe turned his bike around and pedaled the roaring baseball card engine away.

Billy's mouth about hit the ground. Three hundred dollars! That's how much I've made since the start of summer break, he thought to himself.

In an effort to see what the business was worth, Billy immediately reached for his little brown book where he kept track of his daily sales and costs. As he jotted down his assets, his smile grew to epic proportions.

$300 from previous sales sitting in my piggy bank
(That's mine. He's obviously not getting that!)

$30 for the nice card table and chairs
$15 for the Mickey Mouse pitcher
$10 worth of lemonade mix
$30 worth of good golf balls
$85 = total value of business

"What an idiot!" Billy muttered under his breath. "This thing is only worth $85 and he's willing to buy it for $300. If I sell it right now, I can make the other $300 I would have earned by working the rest of the summer. Holy banana bread, I'm going to have $600. I'll be rich!"

That night, Billy decided to give Joe a call to negotiate the deal. As Joe's mother answered the phone, Billy asked to talk with his friend.

When Joe got on the phone, he immediately started the conversation with, "Billy, I'm not paying a dime more than $300." Before Billy could even reply, Joe continued, "And the other part of the deal is I can use your parents' property as long as I want."

Within a split second, Billy could tell Joe was obviously prepared for his phone call. Not knowing how to respond to his demands, Billy defensively said, "Well, I'm going to have to think about it. Bye." Without flinching, Billy immediately hung up the phone like a big-city lawyer.

As Billy turned away from the phone, hung on the kitchen wall, his father, George, raised his hand. With the roles reversed, Billy's father acted like the student while his son was the pretend teacher.

As George remained mute with his hand in the air, Billy muttered a long and drawn-out, "What, Dad?"

George, a man known for carefully choosing his words, said, "Excuse me, what are we doing?"

Billy slowly lifted his hanging head. As he began to speak, he gradually added more enthusiasm in an effort to "sell" his inquisitive father. "Joe offered to buy my lemonade business for $300 and…and…and it's only worth $85! I'm going to have $600. Can you believe that, Dad? Huh? Can ya?"

Without responding, George lowered his hand and spun around in his chair. Billy remained motionless with wide eyes and an expression of confusion. George carefully placed a piece of paper on the table. "All right, son. What is the intrinsic value of your business?" George said quietly.

Excited with his father's willingness to help with kid business, Billy reached into his blue jean pocket to pull out his little brown notebook. As Billy flipped to the page where he recently conducted his math, he stopped and looked at his dad and said, "What's the word 'intrinsic' mean, Dad?"

Anxious to answer Billy's question, George said, "It means

real or genuine." Shrugging his shoulders, Billy said, "Oh, OK," as he pointed to the $85 figure written in his book.

As George reviewed Billy's simple math, he smiled and said, "OK, so what's the intrinsic value?"

Confused, Billy said, "It's $85."

Quick to teach Billy a life lesson, George said, "No, $85 is your book value, or the value of your business if you ended it today. The intrinsic value is always worth more than your book value if you have a profitable business."

As Billy looked at his father with a confused look on his face, George eloquently described the fundamentals to his son with the paper and pen. "Billy, right now you are 12 years old, but how long do you plan on running your lemonade stand?"

"I don't know, probably until I'm 16. I really want to have a car," he exclaimed.

"OK, perfect," his father replied as he started writing on a piece of paper.

The rest of this summer	$300
Next summer (age 13)	$600
The following summer (age 14)	$600
Final summer (age 15)	$600
	Total: $2,100

Intrinsic Value	$2,100
versus	
Book Value	$85
versus	
Current Market Price	$300 — This was Joe's offer to buy everything

"Here, son, look at this," George said as he tilted the paper for Billy to read.

As Billy reviewed the paper, a mix of emotions filled the young child's mind. After a little hesitation he said, "Wow, I could be a thousandaire."

As Billy and his father laughed, George concluded with, "OK, Billy, so do you still want to sell your business?"

"No way," Billy quickly responded.

* * *

As you review the story about Billy's lemonade stand, you quickly realize that owning a business involves math. Math is the centerpiece to properly valuing a business or stock. When Billy was approached with an offer to sell his business, his immediate reaction was "what's it worth?" If figuring out the value of a $100 lemonade stand is important, you can quickly acknowledge that knowing the value of a 10 billion dollar business is exponentially important. Remember the phrase "what's it worth?" It's the keystone to becoming wealthy.

One of the greatest misconceptions with a stock is that it's not a business. Never forget this verbal equation:

Stock = A Real Business

For reasons that are impossible to explain, a majority of people don't value individual shares the same way they value an entire business. This is where Warren Buffett separates himself from the typical investor. Warren Buffett always looks at the ownership of one share in the same light as owning the entire business. Mr. Buffett is famous for never looking at a stock's trading price on the market. Instead, he always tries to determine what HE thinks the company is worth before looking at the price others are willing to sell the company for (the market price).

Before we learn how to value a business, we first must learn more fundamental concepts about stocks. In this section, you learned four key terms:

Earnings: This is the net income after receiving funds and paying debts. For Billy, he earned $600 a summer. So after he paid for his ingredients and cups and collected all the money from his sales, he earned $600 a summer.

Market Price: This is what people in the market are currently willing to buy and sell a stock for. In the story, this was Joe's offer to buy the company for $300.

Book Value: This is the value of the business if it stopped production or work right now. In the story, if Billy stopped work, he would only be able to sell his equipment. Therefore, his company's book value was $85.

Intrinsic Value: This is the value smart investors calculate the business to be worth. The point of this entire book is to learn how to calculate this number. In the story, Billy's father suggested the intrinsic value was $2,100. As you'll find out later in the book, the intrinsic value isn't definitive but does provide a calculative glimpse into potential returns. For example, there is no guarantee that Billy will work for the next three years and earn that amount of money. With that said, there's a strong possibility that this estimate will be accurate.

In order to learn more fundamentals, let's go to the next section and learn more about Billy's future business decisions.

Section 2

Like any neighborhood, every kid on the block heard about Billy and Joe's argument. In fact, Joe was constantly telling every kid in the neighborhood how much money Billy was making from the lemonade stand. In only a few days, Billy was having so many kids approach him about becoming partners that he wanted to scream.

In an effort to fix the problem, Billy went to his financial advisor.

That evening, as his father's blue Ford truck pulled into the driveway, Billy sprinted out of the house and stood at the door like a puppy ready to fetch a bone. As the door carefully opened, Billy began, "Dad, everyone on the block is driving me crazy. They all want to be partners in the business. What do I do?"

As George grabbed his briefcase and exited the vehicle, he didn't say anything. As he walked toward the front door, Billy chased behind him like a kite. "Dad, Dad, Dad, you've got to help me, it's been a really stressful day!" Billy exclaimed.

George, stretching his arms after having worked a 14-hour day, said, "All right Billy, let's figure this out."

Like clockwork, George returned to his paper and pencil teachings. "OK, so how much do you think the market price of your business should be?" George said.

With a look of confusion on his face, Billy said, "Well, you told me it was worth $2,100."

"No," his father quickly corrected, "I said the intrinsic value was that much. May I also remind you that this figure also involves you working every summer for the next three years."

With yet another confused look on his face, Billy said, "Dad, quit talking over my head."

As George laughed, he bluntly said, "Billy the market price is what you'd be willing to sell the business for right now. For example, if all your friends walked through the door right now and said, 'Billy, we'll buy your lemonade stand for $1,000,' would you do it?"

After a long pause, Billy blurted out a quick and thunderous, "Yep!"

With a grin on his face, George said, "OK, then that's your market price."

"Now this is where things become fun," George said to Billy. "You know why?"

"Why's that, Dad?" Billy replied.

"Because you're now going to sell your lemonade stand for $1,000. You're happy, your friends are happy, and everyone wins."

In a rage of frustration, Billy said, "Dad, Joe refused to

pay more than $300. No one else in the neighborhood would ever match that high of a price. How could I possibly sell it for $1,000?"

Without even hesitating, George replied, "Patience and knowledge, Billy."

The next day, Billy was all alone at his lemonade stand selling his profitable drink and golf balls.

After finishing with some customers, three of his friends approached his card table. "Billy, are you going to let us be partners yet or what?"

As Billy turned around with a smile on his face, he said, "Gentlemen, today is your lucky day. Before you are the shares to my business." As the three friends looked down at his table, they saw a box full of small pieces of paper that read:

Looking up in amazement, Billy's friends said, "What in the world is that?"

Carefully rehearsed, Billy started his pitch. "Each piece of paper in the box represents an equal portion of my business. As you can see, I currently own all the pieces of paper. I'm willing to sell each piece of paper for one dollar. At the end of the summer, all the people who own a piece of paper will meet at my house to collect their earnings."

As the three future investors' eyes grew wide with excitement, they quickly countered with, "So, what's the catch?"

Already prepared for the negativity, Billy pointed to the

back of the box where he posted the rules to the business. He read, "Here's my promise. First, I will not make any more pieces of paper than what you see in the box. Second, I will proportionately pay all owners at the end of the summer based on the number of shares they own. Third, I will continue working the business until someone else owns more pieces of paper. At that point, that person will assume the duties of my job." As all three kids looked at Billy like he was a complete idiot for selling pieces of his incredible business, they started reaching for their velcro wallets.

Rumors about Billy selling pieces of his cash-king business spread throughout the neighborhood like wildfire. Needless to say, he was selling shares of his business all day long. At the end of the first day, Billy looked into his "owners" box to see how many shares were left. Although many were sold, the box still looked full. Unable to control his emotions, he started laughing out loud. Billy was laughing because his dad was right. He was slowly selling his business for $1,000.

"Patience and knowledge," Billy muttered under his breath.

In an effort to keep accountability of all the money, Billy reached for his little brown book. Inside the book he had kept a log of all the new owners throughout the day. The log read:

Earl	15 shares
Nancy	10 shares
Jon	10 shares
Stefanie	15 shares
Gwen	3 shares
Demi	2 shares
Joe	45 shares (turns out he didn't even have $300)
My friends' total # of shares	100 shares
My shares (the ones still in the box)	900 shares
Total # of shares outstanding	1,000 shares

After confirming his math four times, Billy looked at his two cigar boxes on the card table. Just like his dad recommended, Billy was now working with two money boxes: one for his lemonade sales and one for all the money he earned from selling the shares to his business. With uncontrollable excitement, Billy opened his new cigar box that held the 100 dollars from the sale of his business. As he stacked the money in neat piles, he looked at the two twenty-dollar bills with a grin on his face. Billy knew the twenties came from Joe. Although Joe was one of Billy's best friends, he shook his head in amazement that "genius" Joe was now buying the business for $1,000 instead of $300.

* * *

What just happened? How was Billy able to morph his business into $1,000 by merely turning it into smaller pieces, or shares? Let's start with identifying the facts surrounding the story.

Everyone can agree that every kid in the neighborhood thought Billy had a good business. Because a one-dollar share was more affordable than purchasing Billy's entire business, kids were willing to become partners in what they perceived as a good thing and a good deal. Once the business was sliced into a bunch of shares, the kids no longer cared about what it was worth. They just wanted to be partners in his profitable business.

Candidly viewing both sides of any story can resolve a lot of ambiguity. Fortunately for intelligent investors, adults are exactly like kids. How many times have you watched a friend purchase a stock simply because "it's a great company?" When I hear people say that phrase in reference to their investment strategy, I almost start convulsing. That phrase is the hallmark of a person destined to lose money in the stock market.

In the story, Billy divided his company into 1,000 pieces, or shares. After selling the shares to the kids in the neighborhood, Billy still owned 90% of the business. Since he still owned 90% of the business, he's entitled to 90% of the earnings. As you can see, the lesson we learned from Section 1 is vitally important.

If the children would have valued each share as if they were buying the whole business, they would have discovered Billy's market valuation of $1,000.

The key term learned in this section was:

Shares Outstanding: This is the number of shares that a company is divided into. For Billy's business, his shares outstanding were 1,000.

Now let's see how Billy's investors like their first earnings meeting.

Section 3

It was the last day of summer break and all of Billy's investors anxiously awaited his owners' meeting. As the kids promptly waited in the living room for Billy to bring their money, he first came out with his box of shares.

"OK, everyone. Like I promised, it's payday. I really appreciate the help everyone provided throughout the summer since we are all owners of the lemonade stand."

With a quick nod from all the kids, Joe quickly said, "OK, so how much is everyone getting?"

Without delaying, Billy replied, "Great question, Joe. In order to figure that out, we first need to write down how many shares each person has."

Quick to volunteer, Nancy said she'd be the secretary and keep notes. As she got a piece of paper and pencil, Demi was quick to announce that she only had two shares of the business. Following Demi's lead, each kid then announced how many shares he or she possessed as Nancy wrote the number next to each child's name. At the end of the tally, everyone still had the same number of shares they initially purchased forty-five days earlier. The only person who didn't announce his shares was Billy.

As all the kids looked at Billy holding the box full of shares, Joe was quick to shout, "Hey, Billy, how many shares do you have?"

Billy, playing dumb, said, "I have no idea. We probably need to count them."

Billy's ploy was an attempt to remain innocent in his secret that he was selling the business for $1,000. Without restraint, Joe ripped Billy's box of shares from his hands and dumped hundreds of shares onto the living room floor. Once on the floor, the kids realized Billy owned a whole lot of shares.

As Joe's frustration increased, Gwen decided to be the great appeaser and say, "OK, guys, let's count Billy's shares and divide up the money."

As the kids counted every single share, they realized Billy owned 900 shares and, therefore, 90% of the business. After counting the last share, they all slowly looked at Billy standing in the corner of the room.

Smiling, Billy tried to divert their anger. "Can you believe we made $300 during the last 45 days?"

After a long pause and awkward silence, Demi innocently said, "Billy, how much money do I get for my two shares?"

Quick to satisfy one of his fellow owners, Billy ran to the kitchen for his calculator. As he walked back into the living room, he said, "This is just like one of those percent problems we learned about in school." As Billy remembered his lessons from math class, he simply took Demi's shares divided by the total number of shares to get the percent she owned of the business. After calculating the percent she owned, he simply multiplied the percent by the $300 in earnings. As Billy hit enter on his calculator, he realized Demi earned $0.60. Before announcing Demi's earnings to the group, he did the same math for each of his friends on a piece of paper.

Name	% of Business x	Earnings	Dividend
Earl	15/1000	$300.00	$4.50
Nancy	10/1000	$300.00	$3.00
Jon	10/1000	$300.00	$3.00
Stefanie	15/1000	$300.00	$4.50
Gwen	3/1000	$300.00	$0.90
Demi	2/1000	$300.00	$0.60
Joe	45/1000	$300.00	$13.50
Billy	900/1000	$300.00	$270.00

Total Dividends	$300.00

As Billy conducted the math, Joe closely watched every calculation over Billy's shoulder. Once Joe realized he would only receive $13.50 for 45 days of work, he was fuming.

"Billy, how can you possibly take $45 from me and only give me a measly $13.50 in return?" Joe said. "I even volunteered to help every day after I became an owner."

As Joe's voice became louder, everyone in the room became uncomfortable.

As if rubbing salt in the wound, Billy corrected Joe, saying, "You mean partial owner."

Barely able to control his emotions, Joe said, "I want my $45 back, Billy!"

Despite Joe's aggressive nature, Billy stuck to his guns. "Joe, you big baby. I can't help it that you didn't properly value your investment in the company. You know those shares are good for the next three years, so stop making me look like the bad guy."

As Joe and Billy yelled louder and louder, the six other kids grew increasingly more worried about their money.

Refusing to believe Billy's response, Joe said, "Billy, you thief. I want to sell my shares back. I no longer want to be a 'PARTIAL' owner."

Slow and deliberate, Billy already had a response for Joe's demand. Billy poignantly said, "Fine, you big jerk, I'll buy your shares back for 70 cents each."

Angry and excited, Joe couldn't believe Billy was actually going to pay him for the 45 pieces of notebook paper he held in his hand.

In an effort to avoid Billy changing his mind, Joe said, "All right, big shot, then prove it."

Without hesitation, Billy pulled out his calculator and multiplied Joe's 45 shares by the 70 cents he promised to pay for each slip of paper. When Billy hit enter on the calculator, he didn't even announce the total amount. Instead, he simply started counting the money he would pay for Joe's shares.

As Billy and Joe exchanged assets, one would have thought the transaction was done at gunpoint. Both children, untrusting of each other, slowly then quickly passed their money and shares. Quick to count the cash, Joe began thumbing through the money like a Las Vegas casino teller. As Joe completed the audit, he looked up at Billy in complete amazement.

Turning to face the six innocent kids in the living room, Joe held $45 in the air ($13.50 for the earnings and $31.50 for the resale of his 45 shares. Remember, Joe invested $45 to start with.)

"As you can see, Billy's a fake," Joe exclaimed. "I hold before you the same $45 I had at the beginning of the summer. Get out while you can," Joe said to the remaining children.

As Joe ran out of the house, the rest of the kids looked terrified. They really didn't understand what happened, but they did know Joe was very upset. By Billy's reaction, it appeared as if Joe had been taken advantage of. Following Joe's lead, the rest of the kids filed in line, demanding their 70 cents per share.

After all the kids departed Billy's home (holding the same amount of money they originally invested), Billy was worried that selling all those shares would have taken away a lot of his money. In order to confirm any losses, Billy opened both cigar boxes to count his money. The old box, which held the money from his earnings, had $270. The new box, which held the money from the sale of his shares, had $30 in it. Billy thought How in the world do I still have $300? Moreover, how did I get all my shares back?

That night, Billy explained the horrible experience to his father. He went into excruciating detail describing everyone's emotions and opinions.

At the end of Billy's rant, George smiled and said, "So, did you learn something?" Rolling his eyes and responding with a long-drawn-out "Daaaaaddddd," George could tell Billy wasn't in the mood for a lecture.

* * *

Reviewing the hundreds of lessons that can be drawn from such a basic story, I'll only focus on the essentials. First, I'll talk about the idea of financial relativity. I would argue this concept is one of the major reasons people lack the patience to accumulate assets. To prove my point, answer the following question: Is the following comparison a synonym (meaning same) or antonym (meaning opposite)?

$1,500,000 : $200,000 $23.00 : $3.06

Most people look at these figures and have a difficult time comparing the numbers. They might assess the figures like this: $1,500,000 – that's how much I dream of having some day. $200,000 – that's how much I'd have after working for 4 years and not paying any taxes or expenses. $23 – that's enough for a quarter tank of gas. $3.06 – that's not even enough to buy a coffee at Starbucks.

If you looked at the question and immediately reached for your calculator, you probably answered, "It's a synonym."

Looking at the question from a mathematical standpoint, you can quickly assess that $200,000 is 13% of $1,500,000. Similarly, $3.06 is 13% of $23.00. The comparison is the same.

So what's my point, and how does this example have anything to do with the story? The point is investors should always consider the growth of their assets in relative terms. Looking at Demi's investment of $2, you could quickly assess that her $0.60 dividend payment in 45 days was a 30% yield! As you know, that's an incredible payment for 45 days. The problem for Demi was that she sold her shares for a 30% loss due to market fears. Assessing the situation from a background in financial relativity adds a whole new light to Billy's business. Every kid in the room shared the 30% dividend yield. Understanding that few successful adult businesses pay a 3% dividend yield per year demonstrates the success of the little business.

So why was Joe so dissatisfied with his earnings? For starters, I think everyone can agree that Joe's $13.50 in earnings didn't appear to be nearly the same as Billy's $270 in earnings – especially in the eyes of a child. In Joe's mind, $13.50 was the amount that would buy his favorite toy, whereas $270 was his dream life savings. Looking at this psychological effect from an adult's perspective, you can empathize with Joe when comparing, $1,350 and $27,000! This can be a very valuable lesson for beginners. Although it might feel like you're making no progress with a $13 dividend payment, always remember George's advice: "Patience and knowledge." Instead, view your gains as a percent. Wow, $13 was a 4% gain. That sure beat the heck out of the .05% gain from my savings account.

Assessing Joe's patience further, let's consider more facts. Not making the situation any easier, Joe witnessed the hundreds in earnings but lacked the initial assets to purchase the whole business. Talk about a situation that millions of adults can relate to. Just like Joe, thousands of adults purchase a few shares of companies like Apple, which earns billions every quarter, yet they can't understand why their stock hasn't doubled in value overnight. In an effort to find their needle in a haystack, these same "investors" trade one company to the next in hopes of becoming rich. Teaching patience is a difficult task. With that said, I've found informed investors are able to tackle the behavior easier than others.

I think everyone can agree that simply buying stock in a great company doesn't mean you'll make a profit. Unbeknownst to most, the success of a stock pick heavily relies on the purchase price as much as the productivity of the already-successful business. This idea is the essence of Warren Buffett's three favorite books.

In this section, we learned the following terms:

EPS (Earnings Per Share): In the first section, we learned that the earnings for the entire summer was $600. Since Billy's little investors didn't buy stock until the middle of the summer, their earnings meeting was only for $300. When companies report their financial information, they base the numbers on an annual figure. Since Billy's lemonade stand makes all of its money for the year during the summer, its annual earnings is $600. Since Billy split his company into 1,000 shares, his earnings per share (EPS) is $600 / 1,000 shares = $0.60 per share.

Price-to-Earnings Ratio (P/E Ratio): Although this term was never mentioned in the story, I want to take this opportunity to define this very important number. To calculate the P/E ratio, you'll simply take the market price and divide it by the earnings. When Billy first sold his shares for $1, his P/E ratio would have been the following:

Market Price Per Share = $1.00
Annual Earnings Per Share = $0.60 (this is the EPS we calculated above)

P/E = $1.00 / $0.60 = 1.66

In Section 3, Billy's market price changed when the children got scared. This is when Billy changed the market price to

$0.70 a share. As a result, the P/E changed. Below is the math that proves the new ratio.

$$P/E = \$0.70 / \$0.60 = 1.16$$

So what the heck does that ratio even mean? A lot!

This is everyone's favorite ratio. A great way to understand it is to say the following phrase out loud when you read it:
For every $1.16 I spend buying this company, I can expect $1.00 in earnings a year later.

Ensure you only replace the $1.16 with the company's P/E when you read the above sentence. The $1.00 in earnings at the end of the sentence never changes. This applies for real stocks too. To demonstrate my point, let's use the P/E for General Electric (GE):

The P/E for GE is 15.05, therefore:

For every $15.05 I spend buying this company, I can expect $1.00 in earnings a year later.

As you can see, the higher the P/E goes, the worse the sentence sounds. Remember that justification when you look at "sexy" picks like Facebook (in 2012), as it had a P/E of 100.

Although this number is very important, it's not the only tool we have in our kitbag to value companies. You'll definitely want to understand this ratio though.

Volume: This is the number of shares traded on any given day. If assessing the volume on Billy's IPO (introductory public offering – a fancy way of saying the businesses' first day of selling shares to the public), it would have been 100 shares. The volume remained at zero until his earnings call. On that day, the volume was once again 100 shares because all the kids got scared and sold each share for $0.70.

Dividend and Yield: This is the amount paid to the owners annually. In the story, Billy was paying his dividend at the end of the summer for the time period in which the kids owned the business. As a result, their dividend was only from $300. When you read real financial reports, the dividend rate and yield is based on the projected payments for the entire year. Since Billy's business earns $600 a year and he pays all his earnings out as a dividend (which usually doesn't happen with real businesses), below is the math that corresponds with those terms.

Dividend Rate = Dividend Paid Annually / Total # of Shares

$0.60 = $600 / 1000

The yield is the percent that's paid to the owner based on the current market price. When the children initially purchased their shares, the dividend yield was the following:

Market Price = $1.00
Dividend Rate = $0.60

Yield = Dividend Rate / Market Price Per Share
60% = $0.60 / $1.00

That's an enormous dividend, and you'll never see that in real stock trading. I typically like to see a 3% (or greater) dividend in a stable market.

When the children sold their shares for $0.70 at the end of the story, what effect did that have on the dividend yield? Below is the math.

Market Price = $0.70
Dividend Rate = $0.60

Yield = $0.60 / $0.70 = 85.7%

As you can see, when the price decreases, the dividend yield increases as long as the dividend rate remains constant.

Be sure to really study these terms and understand them. As the book progresses, it builds on the fundamentals taught along the way. You'll find the reading much easier if you don't move forward until you master the lessons taught during each chapter.

In order to help you understand the concepts presented in this book, I've created a website that teaches each chapter by video. If you go to www.BuffettsBooks.com, you'll find the website is broken-down into three courses. If you go to course 1, unit 1, you'll find five lessons that teach the material you just read about. In order to provide a better scope of the material, I use different scenarios, but similar terms and fundamentals. This way you can view the material from numerous vantage points. Each lesson is about 15 minutes long, and I really think it will help you understand the root of each chapter. I would highly recommend watching the video lessons that accompany each chapter before moving forward in the book.

Chapter 2
A Child's First Bond
Bonds 101

As the front door opened, Billy jumped out of his chair. In a quick dash to greet his dad, Billy arrived at the door before his father even got in the house.

"Yes, Billy?" George said.

"Dad, you won't believe what happened on my first day of school," Billy responded.

"You got straight A's on your report card," George jokingly said with a straight face.

"Come on, Dad, it was my first day," Billy said. Ignoring George's joke, Billy quickly continued. "What I wanted to tell you was Joe went to the bank and purchased a savings bond. Can you believe that? Joe said he is going to make all kinds of money with that thing"

As George continued to listen to Billy, he walked into the house and put his briefcase in the closet. After Billy was done barraging his father with questions and statements, George asked his son, "So I'm assuming you want to buy a bond too?"

"Well, yeah, it sounds like a great way for me to make money while I'm in school," Billy replied.

In total amazement of his son's entrepreneurial spirit, George walked into the kitchen and returned with a piece of paper and pencil. George said, "All right, Billy, you first need to understand what a bond is before you just give your money away."

Salivating for information, Billy sat next to his father as he began to teach.

"The first thing you need to understand is a bond is a loan. Essentially, you are lending a person, a business, or a government your money. When you give your money to a person or organization, you establish a bond with them. The bond is an agreement that specifies when and how the organization or person will give you your money back – with interest."

As George continued to teach, Billy patiently listened to every word. "So let's use an example," George said. "Remember at the beginning of the summer when we went to the carnival and you drank the delicious lemonade from the carnival stand?"

Quick to reply, Billy gave an animated, "I sure do."

"OK, great," George replied. "The reason you liked the carnival lemonade so much was because it was freshly squeezed. They had that fancy lemon-squeezing machine that crushed the lemon juice right into your drink. Billy, if you had that machine, do you think you would sell more lemonade?"

"Absolutely," Billy said.

Smiling, George continued. "OK, let's assume the cost of the squeezing machine is $1,000. How do you buy the machine if you only have $900?"

After thinking about the question for a few seconds, Billy innocently said, "Well, I would have to wait until I earned another $100."

Grinning from ear to ear, George thought to himself If only adults could start thinking like kids, they would probably find themselves in a lot less trouble. Leading Billy down the lessons path, he continued. "Well, that's a great answer, but you could also issue a $100 bond. The bond would put the extra hundred dollars in your hands today so you could start making more money with the lemon squeezer tomorrow."

As George described the bond, he drew the following picture on a piece of paper:

Billy's Snack Shack Bond

Face/Par Value: $100
Coupon Rate: 5% Annual

Date of Issue: 1 September 2011

Date of Maturity: 1 September 2012

Coupon 1	Coupon 2
Redeemable on:	Redeemable on:
28 February 2012	1 September 2012
For	For
$2.50	$2.50

As Billy looked at the bond on paper, he scratched his head. Reading Billy's mind, George decided to demonstrate the concept with real money.

As George fetched a hodgepodge of currency from his wallet, he slowly counted $100 in coins and bills. After confirming the amount, George looked at his son and said, "Hello, Billy. I'd like to invest in your company and buy your $100 bond." Without hesitation, George pushed the $100 in cash in front of Billy as he held the paper bond in his hand. As the money sat in front of Billy, his eyes grew large.

"OK, Billy, today is 1 September 2010 and I just purchased your bond. In exchange for my money, you give me your bond," George said.

After the exchange, George continued, "Now, let's fast-forward six months in time. Now it's the 28th of February. As you can see, I'm going to rip this first coupon from the bond and give it to you. In exchange, you give me $2.50." As George ripped off the first coupon, he said, "Billy, you are paying 5% annual interest on $100, so that's why you are paying me $2.50 after the first six months."

After completing the first transaction, George and Billy warped through time again and assumed it was 1 September 2012 – one year after the purchase of the bond. As a result, they did the same transaction for the second coupon; Billy handed George another $2.50.

After the exchange of the second coupon, George held up the $5 he received from the two coupons. "This $5 is the 5% interest you paid to borrow my $100 for the past year." As Billy and George looked at the paper bond, George showed Billy where the bond read "Coupon rate: 5% annual." After reading the rate, George told his son that most coupons are paid to the bondholder twice a year.

As George and Billy continued looking at the bond, George said, "OK, as you can see in our example, it is the 1st of September 2012. This means your bond is also mature. As a result, you also need to repay my $100."

As Billy looked down at his pile of money his father gave him for the initial purchase of the bond, he realized there was only $95 remaining. As George looked at his son, he said, "Do you get it?"

Smiling, Billy shouted, "I sure do!"

* * *

Although this short and simple chapter really simplifies the ownership of bonds, the fundamentals of how they work are what I want you to understand. Purchasing a bond is nothing more than a way for you to loan money to a company or government. As you'll find in the second portion of this book, there are advantages and disadvantages for all sorts of bond investments. As you grow in your depth of knowledge, never forget the following:

Purchasing a Bond = Providing a Loan

Looking at purchasing a bond from the perspective of a lender, you'll quickly realize there are a lot of rational and intuitive things you need to consider – so think like a bank lender.

If you would like to watch the three video lessons that accompany this chapter on www.BuffettsBooks.com, simply navigate to Course 1, Unit 2.

Note: A Treasury bill matures in 1 year or less. A treasury note matures in 1 to 10 years. A Treasury bond matures in 20 or more years. In the story, the correct terminology for Billy's debt obligation should have been a bill. In an effort to maintain consistency with bond valuation in the second part of the book, I refer to the asset as a bond.

Chapter 3
The Lake
Markets 101

I t was the first day of the next year's summer break and Billy couldn't be angrier. Although most kids his age would have been thrilled to be going on a family vacation to Pymatuning Lake, Billy was not. For the entire school year, Billy anxiously awaited the opening of his beloved lemonade stand. Instead of sitting on the golf course with his fresh cup-blown lemonade, Billy was instead sitting in between his parents on the way to Pymatuning Lake. Billy had never been to a lake, and he couldn't understand why people would want to swim in a dark and unclean pool of water.

"Dad, why are we going to the lake on my first day off?" Billy questioned.

A little annoyed, George sternly replied, "Billy, did you know this is the only time of year I get to take an entire week off?"

After George expressed his frustration, the rest of the car ride was quiet. Billy knew better than to provoke his father with more complaining.

Once the family arrived at the lake, Billy's anger quickly changed to restrained excitement. Unbeknownst to him, Billy's father had a close friend who owned a cottage situated directly on Pymatuning Lake. The frustration of Billy's parents was quickly alleviated as they watched their complaining son immediately change his attitude and sprint for the dock.

As Billy ran halfway through the yard, he saw another boy emerge from a boat that was being tied to the dock. Stopping in the grass to understand what was happening, Billy turned and looked at his parents to ensure he was allowed to proceed. With a quick pause and look of reassurance, George pushed his hands toward his son to signal his approval.

With lightning speed, Billy arrived at the shore and helped tie the boat to the dock. As Billy finished helping the family secure the boat, the other young boy introduced himself.

With pure excitement, the boy said, "Hey, my name is Gary. What's yours?"

Before Billy could respond, George interrupted the kid conversation and greeted his adult friend. After shaking hands and briefly discussing their travels, George introduced both families. After the brief introduction, Billy gleamed with excitement. He didn't realize he would be spending the entire week with another boy the same age.

As the adults walked away, Gary and Billy remained on the dock and continued their conversation. As expected, the children covered almost all adolescent subjects. The two boys truly enjoyed each other's company, considering they both lacked siblings. Like most boys, they quickly found amusement in skipping rocks off the end of the dock. As the boys flung countless amounts of stones into the water, Billy was startled by a school of fish passing underneath the dock.

"Holy moly, look at all those fish," Billy exclaimed.

As Gary walked to the side of the dock where Billy was looking, Gary said, "Yeah, they always do that. What's the big deal."

As Billy tried to think of a witty response to his comment, Gary grabbed a stone and prepared to launch the small rock into the water. As Billy looked up, he could see Gary was aiming at the school of fish. Before Billy could even stop him, Gary pitched a rock at all the fish.

As the stone impacted the water, Billy was mesmerized by what he saw. Initially, he felt bad for the creatures, but after watching every last fish disperse immediately, Billy started to laugh.

"How in the world did they all know to swim away?" Billy questioned.

Shrugging his shoulders, Gary said, "I don't know. They

just got scared."

As the two boys continued to play on the dock, they saw different schools of fish pass beneath them. In an effort to solve the mystery, Billy began to experiment.

As the next school of fish passed beneath the dock, Billy reached for a really small stone. He was curious to know if a smaller threat would still scare the entire school. Instead of throwing the projectile, Billy delicately dropped the stone in the center of the school. As he watched the rock penetrate the water's surface, he was again stunned. Like before, the fish instantly scattered from the tiny pebble.

Looking up at Gary with a huge grin on his face, Billy shouted, "Totally awesome!"

As the week progressed, the two boys really enjoyed their time at the lake. They spent countless hours in the water and on the boat. Since it was Billy's first time in a body of water that wasn't a public swimming pool, he remained mesmerized by the fish. Almost any opportunity Billy had to discuss the fish, he took advantage of. As the week progressed, George fielded all kinds of fish questions. He told Billy how the fish live during the winter months and attempted to explain why they like the taste of worms. After a few days of fielding Billy's countless questions, George thought of the perfect place to take his son.

That afternoon, after lunch, George loaded Billy into the car and drove him to a pier. As they were on their way, Billy inquisitively asked his father, "Dad, where are we going?"

With a brief pause, George said, "I'm taking you to where all the fish are."

With an animated response, Billy shouted, "Cool!" After a minute of silence he said, "Can we throw rocks at them?"

Barely able to control his laughter, George replied, "Yeah, I've got a few cinderblocks in the trunk."

Astounded by his father's reply, Billy shouted, "Holy macaroni and cheese, this is going to be awesome."

Laughing even harder, George simply looked at Billy and

rubbed the top of his son's head. As the two arrived at a large deck overlooking the water, Billy was mesmerized at what he saw. With more than a dozen people throwing food into the water, Billy saw well over a thousand fish all fighting at the surface for a scrap of food.

"Oh, my goodness. Why are all those fish here?" Billy questioned.

Not wasting any time, George said, "Because they want a free lunch."

As Billy looked at the countless number of carp flopping on the surface, he said, "How do they all know to come here?"

Thinking about Billy's question for a second, George replied, "Out of instinct. One fish can see his friend getting free food, so he starts looking in the same spot. After a few fish get fed, every fish in the lake starts getting greedy. They all want the free food."

Astounded by the number of fish fighting for food, Billy couldn't stop laughing and staring at the amazing sight. There were so many fish that it looked like a person could walk across the water on the backs of the fish.

After a couple of minutes, Billy looked at his dad and said, "You know, Dad, if I were a fish, I'd be out in the middle of the lake."

Smiling, George said, "Why's that, Billy?"

With his arms pointing at all the fish, Billy replied, "Look at all those fish. If they are all right here, think about all the food that's not getting eaten out there." As Billy finished his sentence, he pointed toward the middle of the lake about a mile away.

Amazed at his son's brilliance, George said, "You're probably right, Billy. I'm sure it's easy pickins out there."

* * *

After reading this short and somewhat bizarre story, you might be wondering what it has to do with investing. Well, let's start with three key words that described the fish Billy studied: instinct, fear, and greed. These three words are why informed investors can make money in the stock and bond markets.

Like fish, humans are equipped with numerous instincts. As you might expect, most of these instincts revolve around survival. For example, if you were standing on a city street and a large crowd of people started running directly toward you, how would you react? Naturally, you would turn in the same direction and start running. You wouldn't need to be told by the crowd that something bad was going to happen. Instead, your ability to discern the opinion of the group would be enough to conclude that something scary was about to happen. As a result, you would follow the crowd's lead.

In the story, when Gary threw a rock at the school of fish, how many fish were actually threatened by the projectile? If you answered one or two, you would be right. With such a small number of fish actually being threatened, how many swam away? That's right, all of them. This is a very important characteristic to understand. How many times in financial markets do investors sell their shares because they are scared of the unknown? Often. They are the small fish who see the big ones moving out. Instead of looking above the water to where the rock is being thrown, they are focused on the tails of the fish in front of them; they move when others move. As you continue reading this book, my goal is to teach you to stop looking at the other fish and start identifying the rocks being thrown in the water. (As you learn later, getting hit by the rock typically means you've invested in companies that carry a lot of debt.)

Turning back to the first chapter, you can quickly draw a parallel between the instinct of the fish and Billy's friends. In the story, when Billy started selling shares of his lemonade stand, the kids of the neighborhood flocked to the investment for a "free lunch." The kids initially found comfort in owning shares because everyone on the block shared the opinion that easy money was going to be made. This mutual opinion of the group provided comfort to the children as they purchased the shares of the lemonade stand, therefore allowing them to forget about the calculable value of the investment.

Equally important, let's examine the fear instinct. If I asked which child symbolically represented the tail of the big fish that was swimming away, who would you guess? If you said Joe, you would be correct. It's obvious now that the 30% gain in 45 days was an outstanding deal for the children, but we all know they still sold all their shares. As you can see, the instinct of fear determined the children's decision to sell their profitable business – not value.

The most startling aspect of this example is that most educated adults still fall victim to the fear and greed instincts outlined above. Everyone in America knows the saying "Buy low and sell high," but how many people actually live by it? I mean, seriously, how many people did you know during the darkest days of the 2008 recession who were actively investing large amounts of money in stocks? Probably not that many.

For informed investors, fear and greed cycles are enormous opportunities. Secretly, billionaires start to salivate during the peaks and valleys of these cycles; they truly are the lifeblood of their existence. Ironically, this is how billionaires perceive market trends during volatile times:

Stocks

During Fear Cycles (Recessions): These are the least risky and most profitable times for purchasing stock.

During Greed Cycles (Bull Markets): These are the most risky and least profitable times for purchasing stocks.

Bonds

During Fear Cycles (Recessions): These are the most risky and least profitable times for purchasing bonds.

During Greed Cycles (Bull Markets): These are the least risky and most profitable times for purchasing bonds.

You might be asking why the opinions of wealthy investors are the opposite of the public. The answer is simple: wealthy investors always understand the intrinsic value of their investments. As a result, they never let the market value (or opinions of the masses) affect their decisions. Looking at this assessment, you can now understand why Warren Buffett is quoted as saying, *"Be fearful when others are greedy, and greedy when others are fearful."*

Here is a simple rule I live by:

Market price is never equal to intrinsic value (which is the antithesis of the 1863 French economist Jules Regnault's Efficient Market Hypothesis).

If the following rule is true, a conclusion can be deduced.

Relatively speaking, stocks and bonds are either profitable or unprofitable. The amount depends on which side and magnitude the market value falls, at any given point in time, from the assessed intrinsic value of the security.

As a result, investment opportunities can be made if you can calculate the intrinsic value of an investment and compare it to the market prices. (Don't worry. Part II of this book will teach you how to reasonably assess the intrinsic value of stocks and bonds.)

To put this idea into terms that everyone can understand, let's look back to chapter 1 and review Joe's investing options:

Since Joe only had 45 dollars to invest, let's look at how he could have employed that capital.

Investment #1 (Savings Bond): Joe could have invested his money in a 3% savings bond at the bank. After 1 year, Joe's $45 would turn into $46.35.

Investment #2 (Billy's Company): Joe could purchase 45 shares of Billy's business. Each share would produce $0.60 in earnings per year. After 1 year, if Joe could sell his shares for the same price he purchased them for, his investment would be worth $72. (*Note: In the story, the children only received $0.30 per share in the earnings meeting because it was only for half the summer.)

Now, looking at this very generic scenario, we can quickly see that investment #2 was a much better choice for making money. So let's put a twist on the scenario. Let's assume the savings bond is still earning 3% a year, but Billy is really greedy and he's selling his shares for a much higher price – let's say $20 a share (instead of only $1). Based on this price, let's see how Joe's investment in Billy's business changes in value.

As a result of Billy's expensive $20/share market price, Joe can only buy 2.25 shares with his $45.

Since the earnings for the company remain the same for the year – $600, and there's still 1,000 shares outstanding – Joe's cut is still $0.60 a share. Since he owns 2.25 shares, and each share still makes $0.60 a year, that means Joe will make $1.35. This means his $45 investment will turn into $46.35 after the first year.

As you can see, the more expensive price of Billy's shares produced the same return as the zero-risk savings bond! Based on those circumstances, I think everyone can agree the savings bond is a much better deal because it has no risk. You see, when the seller is greedy (i.e., Billy selling the shares for $20 each), the risk goes up.

This example was provided to demonstrate the constant comparison that investors must make in order to properly value their assets. In this basic and quick scenario, you saw the same business with the same earnings completely change in value based on the market price. Although you might think a company couldn't change in value this much, you might be surprised how many companies can swing in market price during good and bad economies. The fear and greed cycle is alive and well all throughout our financial markets. Your job is to find the quality companies (like Billy's lemonade stand) that are selling for $1 and not $20.

Great investors always think for themselves. Never let the opinions of the masses sway the calculative value you place on your investments.

If you would like to watch the three video lessons that accompany this chapter on www.BuffettsBooks.com, simply navigate to course 1, unit 3.

Chapter 4
George's Final Guidance
The Connection

It was the start of Billy's senior year in high school. His days of lemonade selling and competing with neighbors were far behind him. Although he was always looking for ways to make money, most of his time was spent chasing women and shining cars.

One day while Billy was polishing his car, George walked out of the house and approached his son. George was carrying a briefcase and seemed to be on his way to take care of some business.

"Where are you going, Dad?" Billy asked.

"I'm off to the bank. Would you like to come?" George questioned. As he paused and waited for Billy's reply, he changed his inquiry into a statement. "On second thought, get in the car. You'll thank me later," George said with a serious look on his face.

As Billy and his father got into the car, George said, "Do you know what's happening in the news, Billy?"

"Um, the Steelers are playing really well," Billy jokingly replied.

Looking at Billy with a grimace on his face, George began to speak. "Right now, our country is going through a very large recession. I'm on my way to the bank to sell my bonds so I can use the money to purchase really cheap stocks. Do you know what everyone else in the country is doing?"

After a little thought, Billy answered, "The exact opposite."

Smiling, George replied with animation, "That's right, son! They are doing the exact opposite."

As George got more excited, Billy could tell his father wasn't focused on driving. He was missing stop signs and never even put on his turn signals.

"You see, Billy, right now, people are fearful. As a result, I'm reacting to that fear and I'm selling my conservative fixed-income securities – or bonds. The reason I'm selling my long-term bonds is because I can charge an enormous premium on the price. You see, I bought these 30-year bonds for $1,000 each only 3 years ago. These bonds pay 6% interest every year. Right now, everyone is scared about the economy, and I can sell each bond for $1,432. If people were going to buy a bond today, the best rate they could get is 3.5%. Because that's the best rate, and I'm sitting on a 6% bond, I can charge $1,432 for each."

As George was talking, Billy looked at his father in amazement. His dad wasn't scared. He seemed so sure and confident.

"Now Billy, what I'm teaching you is the vicious cycle of the redistribution of wealth around the country. Right now, during these horrible economic times, the wealthy are becoming wealthier and, unfortunately, the poor are becoming poorer. Your future ability to react to the conditions will soon determine your fate.

"Now, let's take a step back and consider how I got in this position today," George stated. "Three years ago, our country was experiencing an enormous boom in the stock market. Everyone in this country was buying stock like dogs chasing a meat wagon. Billy, do you know what I was buying during those great times?"

A little confused, Billy shrugged his shoulders.

Looking down at the briefcase, George paused and said, "Those bonds right there. I could have been following the crowd of greedy investors and buying stocks, but I knew they were overvalued. As a result, bonds were actually a better investment despite the opinions of most people."

As George gave Billy a few seconds to comprehend the whole scenario, he could see the gerbils running in his son's head. After a long pause Billy spoke.

"All right, I understand the principle of being greedy when others are fearful and vice versa, but how do you know when others are being greedy?"

Struck by Billy's understanding, George got excited as he placed the vehicle in park at the bank. Turning to face Billy, George said, "It's easy. You simply compare your expected return of a stock to the expected return of a long-term bond. Whichever has the higher return is the one you buy."

Looking at his father with a little skepticism, Billy said, "Dad, how do you figure that stuff out?"

"Son, you need to know how to calculate the difference," George said. "There are plenty of investors who have consistently made millions through patience and a conservative strategy. The only way you'll ever know is to start with the basics and teach yourself."

PART II
Teaching Yourself

The first part of this book was written in a manner to provide you with the basic tools to understand stocks, bonds, and the market. It was meant to encourage you by providing everyday stories that anyone can understand. Although I could continue providing anecdotal stories throughout the rest of the book, I feel it would detract from the total value I could add to your knowledge as an investor. Unfortunately, not everything with stock investing is intuitive. As a result, the rest of the book is somewhat disjointed from the first portion of elementary learning. In order to compensate for my skipping ahead, I would like to bring up an idea that is very near and dear to my heart: taking the initiative.

As a member of the military, one of the things I had beat into my head at the U.S. Military Academy was the idea of taking the initiative. On my first day of class, I was taught a whole new method of learning – nothing like what I was taught in high school. This method of learning was called the Thayer method. Essentially, as students – or cadets – we were forced to teach ourselves all the academic lessons before receiving the professional instruction from our teachers. This Thayer method started on day one and didn't end until graduation four years later. This method of learning might sound completely backwards, but its purpose was profound.

By forcing us to teach ourselves, and often take tests before learning lessons, we learned how to take the initiative and learn on our own. I would argue this skill has been an invaluable asset throughout my life as I taught myself new ideas and subjects. As you continue reading the rest of this book, I think you'll find that the difficulty drastically increases from the first portion of the book. This may be attributed to my marginal writing or structure, but I encourage you not to become discouraged.

My intent is not to write a book that frustrates you, but instead one that provides the keys to solving the whole problem. This book is meant to be a small, easy-to-read, single resource as opposed to a large, bulky, drawn-out series of books. Hopefully, if there's something that I miss in this book, it'll be covered on the www.BuffettsBooks.com website. Also, feel free to sign up for the forum found on the website so your difficult questions can get answered there.

If at any time you feel lost or see a term that hasn't been properly described, I highly encourage you to reread the section or conduct online research to understand the missing piece(s) of information. Hopefully, if I've done my job, the important information should all be covered. Like most subjects, missing information can have a compounding effect if not maintained properly.

Chapter 5
How Do We Define Success?

Section 1

Now that we've talked about the fundamentals through Billy's exploits with stocks, bonds, and the manic-depressive nature of the market in which they're traded, we can stop talking about the adventures of Billy and start talking about your investments.

You, as a calm, clear-headed, and logical investor, have an advantage over the rest of the market. Most people treat the market like gambling. They are driven by groupthink, fear, and greed. They often act illogically and without doing their research. This book will describe the basics of value-based research and stock selection. If you will let it, it'll help you invest without fear of the unknown.

When you come into the market to make money, doing what the average investor does is often a story with an unhappy ending. Understand, the market doesn't really produce anything. It is a medium for the exchange of wealth. It's similar to a large poker table. The table isn't producing money for the players; instead, it's merely a location for transferring funds from one player to another. You do not want to take a seat at this poker table until you understand the odds of your plays, what the cards mean, and until you are certain that you are not the sucker at the table. Though the market doesn't really produce anything, it does grow over time as a factor of the businesses and the labor it represents. Thus, ultimately, the average investor does make money. However, responsible and disciplined methods can increase those returns substantially. They can also reduce the chances that a market crash (which historically happens every 6 to 10 years) will result in a personal finance crash or retirement plan crash.

So here is the first question we need to answer: what is the minimum performance an investment should yield to be considered successful? How do we define success? Do we have to beat the market? Do we have to simply retain our present value?

The author of this book contends that the standard for investing (specifically, long term) should be taken from a readily available risk-free investment. What you choose to use is up to you. For the sake of argument here, we will use the 10-year Federal Treasury note as a standard (a method adopted from Benjamin Graham).

The reason the Treasury note is regarded as a foundational standard is because it cannot fail to pay. Credit risk is irrelevant when looking at this bond because the issuer of this bond (the Federal Treasury) can simply print more money. Unlike corporate or municipal bond issuers, the ability to create money makes the Federal Treasury invulnerable to default. Thus, we will consider this bond to be the golden standard for risk-free investing. All other securities will be considered to be of higher risk (unless issued by the Federal Treasury).

The 10-year Treasury note, if purchased today, yields 2.125% per year. That means that a note purchased for $100 would send you a check for $2.13 each year for 10 years before returning your $100. If this Treasury note investment is considered to be risk-free, then why would anyone enter an investment that makes less than 2.125%?

Then, it must make sense that any investment that involves risk and is not expected to return more than the 10-year Federal Treasury note (but which has a similar timeframe) is a bad investment. Why accept risk for a rate of return that can be attained without risk?

This distinction is important because this comparison establishes the basis for responsible decision-making for the enterprising investor. As the market doesn't just consist of stocks and bonds, this discussion gives the responsible investor the groundwork for comparing bonds, stocks, business ventures, and any other investments. Because we now know that we don't want to accept risk for a rate of return less than that of a 10-year Treasury note, we can rule out any business ventures or securities that do not show a substantial chance of exceeding that target minimum rate of return.

I made this realization after several years in a real estate venture in which I roughly broke even. Though I ultimately made a very small monetary gain, the entire venture had to be considered a loss because I could have invested the same funds for a much greater return in Treasury bonds for substantially fewer headaches and no risk. For my venture to have broken even, I'd have needed to get a rate of return equal to what Treasury bonds of the same period would have yielded (and still I'd have accepted unnecessary risk and headache).

Section 2

What is Risk Worth?

Because we now know what our minimum rate of return should be, we now have to ask ourselves a couple questions, namely, why should we accept risk?

So, what makes risk acceptable? In Section 1 of this chapter, we established a minimum acceptable rate of return. We determined that no security should return less than the return of an investment with zero risk (Treasury bond). How much do we have to make in order to justify accepting the risk of purchasing a security that could lose value?

I recommend putting substantial thought into this question. Realize that the first purpose of investing is to protect the initial value of your savings (also known as "principal").

I won't consider an investment unless I think it'll return at least 1.75 times the rate of return I'd expect from a zero-risk investment. I consider the peace of mind of a zero-risk investment to be worth enough to where I won't consider risk for less than that rate of return. This is my decision. I recommend you make your own.

One important thing to keep in mind is that if an investment is considered "high risk," it's not an investment. It's a gamble. The wise investor will never fall for the "high-risk, high-gain" trap. If it seems really risky, it's probably just a bad place for your money.

If you would like to watch the video lesson that accompanies this chapter on www.BuffettsBooks.com, simply navigate to course 2, unit 1.

Chapter 6
Valuing a Bond

From 1928 until 2011, the average stock growth was 11.20% and the average Treasury bond returned 5.41%. From 2002 to 2011, the average stock growth was 4.93% and the average Treasury bond returned 6.85%.

Purchasing bonds is something that most junior investors really never understand or focus on. Part of the reason is most bonds can't be purchased in increments lower than $5,000 a piece (and even that's a low figure in some cases). Although this might be an initial setback for investors with minimal cash, I'll be sure to briefly cover other ways to take advantage of this market.

In this chapter you will learn the following three things:

1. You'll learn why inflation and interest rates are imperative to investing.

2. You'll learn the math equations and techniques for valuing bonds (which you'll need to understand for stock valuation).

3. You'll learn the best way to make bonds part of your investment approach.

So let's start with the information we learned in Part I. A bond is nothing more than a loan. When a company or government wants to raise money, it has the option to issue a bond in order to raise capital. As everyone remembers from their high school history classes, the United States issued war bonds. This was a very easy way for the country to trade a piece of paper for money in order to finance wars. The piece of paper was a debt obligation owed to the holder.

As we go a step beyond the meaning of a bond, you'll quickly find that a few things have an impact on the value of that bond: interest rates, inflation, and the financial health of the issuer.

Interest Rates: One of the federal government's greatest tools in trying to control financial markets is adjusting the interest rate. Although there's a lot of controversy surrounding the purpose and authority of the Federal Reserve, most agree the institution isn't going away. As a result, the federal government will continue to have the ability to adjust interest rates as it deems necessary. So when and why would it want to do that?

Let's assume the country just went through a really bad recession. How do you think the Federal Reserve will adjust interest rates? If you said lower, you'd be exactly right. The reason the Federal Reserve lowers interest rates is because it wants to spark spending in the economy. When people spend money, businesses make more money and citizens have jobs.

Now, let's assume the country is experiencing a really strong bull market (stocks are going way up). Unemployment rates are low and the economy is performing really well. What do you think the Federal Reserve is doing at this point? If you said raising interest rates, you'd be exactly right. One thing I think everyone can agree on is that the leaders of the Federal Reserve absolutely understand macroeconomics. They know that if the stock market and the U.S. economy are growing too quickly, it will lead to a financial bumble. The Fed's mechanism to control this growth is by raising interest rates.

Now that you understand why and when interest rates change, let's quickly look at how the value of a bond adjusts to this movement. I want you to imagine that you've just purchased a $1,000 30-year bond and it pays a 5% annual coupon. This means you'll make 5% on your $1,000 for the next 30 years if you never sell the asset. Now, let's assume we fast-forward in time 1 year later – you still own the 5% bond. At this point, the U.S. economy's unemployment has increased and many people are claiming the country is in a recession. As a result, the Federal Reserve has lowered interest rates, and 30-year bonds are now selling for 4%. In this situation, are you holding a more valuable or less valuable bond? If you answered more valuable, you'd be exactly right.

Since newly issued bonds are only yielding 4% and you've got the 5% bond, you can now sell your security for a premium.

Here's a simple rule to memorize:

When interest rates rise - Your bond values decrease
When interest rates decrease - Your bond values increase

Below is a very important chart that demonstrates how a bond's market price changes with interest rates. I highly recommend you take time to look at this chart carefully because it will demonstrate the importance of never buying a low-coupon, long-term bond. It will also demonstrate the importance of buying a high-coupon, long-term bond. I must highlight that the numbers represented below were based on a 30-year bond that was just issued.

The changing market price of a $1,000 par bond with interest rates:

	2% Interest Rate	3% Interest Rate	4% interest Rate	5% Interest Rate	6% Interest Rate	7% interest rate
2% Bond	1000	803	652	536	446	376
3% Bond	1225	1000	826	691	585	501
4% Bond	1450	1197	1000	845	723	626
5% Bond	1674	1394	1174	1000	862	751
6% Bond	1899	1591	1348	1155	1000	875
7% Bond	2124	1788	1521	1309	1138	1000

As an investor looks at the chart above, it becomes clear

how bond investors make their money: They buy high-coupon bonds when interest rates are high. After acquiring the asset, they continue to collect the coupons until interest rates drop. When that happens, they sell the high-coupon bond for a premium and re-invest the money into new asset(s) that have better returns (most likely a stock at this point).

Note: In 2001, the U.S. government suspended issuing the well-known 30-year Treasury bond. After only four and a half years, it was reissued due to the demand from pension funds and large institutional investors.

Inflation: The next variable that affects the value of your bond is inflation. If there's one thing that's for sure, the U.S. government likes to spend money. What many citizens don't know is that the U.S. government has two ways to pay for that spending. The first is obvious – taxes. The second is sneaky – inflation.

Although I would argue 1% to 3% inflation is a good thing for our economy because it promotes savings, higher inflation is not good. In fact, I'd actually argue that maintained levels higher than 4% are somewhat criminal.

So what causes inflation?

The answer to that question is really easy: inflation occurs because the federal government prints additional money from thin air. That's right, it just prints more money. Now that might sound borderline illegal, but it's obviously not. Now that you understand how it happens, you'll be better equipped to know when it might be used as an instrument to pay national debts, and increase the money supply. Now, let's look at inflation's impact on bonds.

If you owned a bond that paid a 4% coupon and the average inflation over the time you held the bond was 4%, guess how much wealthier you became? You guessed it, you didn't gain a penny! The value of the dollar remained constant.

In simple terms, inflation is nothing more than an acid

that eats away at the value of a bond or loan. When you're calculating the value of your investment, always be sure to assess the impact that inflation will have on a bond.

As you get more advanced with your investing, you'll realize that stocks are somewhat inflation proof. In 1937 a smart Harvard student, John Burr Williams, wrote his doctoral thesis, which was titled *The Theory of Investment Value*. His thesis was published as a book one year later. Although this isn't considered one of Buffett's three favorite books, Buffett does acknowledge Williams' accomplishments and input to value-based investing. One of the concepts that Williams talks about in his classic investing book is the idea that debt-free stocks aren't affected by inflation.

To understand this principle, let's look back at Billy's lemonade stand. In that simple scenario, let's assume inflation increased by 10% from one year to the next. How would Billy have reacted to the devaluation of money? As you might expect, he would have increased the price of his lemonade from $1.00 a cup to $1.10 a cup. Since Billy had to pay more money for his supplies, he had to raise his rates. Instead of eating the additional cost, Billy simply raised the cost of his product and made his customer pay the new cost. In the end, the customer is the person who's affected by the inflation, not the viable business. (The term "viable business" is an important part of this inflation-proof idea). When Billy calculates his year-end earnings, he has still produced the same relative income because he has adjusted the pricing of his product in a manner that accounts for the inflated costs. Although Williams highlights this interesting point in his book, I'd still like to emphasize that a stock that deals with debt will still be affected by inflation. A couple decades later, Benjamin Graham also addressed this idea in The Intelligent Investor. Graham simply emphasizes that inflation doesn't have a positive or negative impact on the value of a stock – therefore confirming Williams' thesis. Be advised, if you're buying a bank stock or a company that carries a lot of debt, this rule will not apply.

TIPS: Since I just talked about inflation, I'm going to quickly mention a Treasury Inflation-Protected Security (TIPS). This type of bond simply protects against the vulnerability of inflation. In order for this to work, the federal government increases and decreases the principal of the TIPS investment at the same rate as inflation. When a TIPS matures, you are paid the adjusted principal or original principal, whichever is greater. If inflation is something you're genuinely worried about (which is a plausible concern), investing in a TIPS bond is a great decision. To learn more about TIPS bonds, go to: http://www.treasury direct.gov.

Financial Health of Issuer: When you go to a bank to apply for a home loan, what is one of the first things the loan officer wants to know? That's right, the financial health of your credit and your earnings capability. The reason the loan officer wants to know is because he doesn't want you to default on the loan. Since loan officers aren't in the business of selling foreclosed homes, they want to ensure that after the house is sold, you have the aptitude to make your payments.

When purchasing a bond, you need to think just like a loan officer. You need to be confident that the company or government you're lending your hard-earned money to has the ability to pay you back with interest.

One of the easiest kinds of bonds to assess is one from the federal government. As we discussed earlier, the Federal Reserve has the ability to simply print more money, and as a result, the Feds will always have the ability to make their payments.

As you look at state and municipal bonds, the financial health of the issuer becomes a lot more questionable. Since these governments don't print their own money, they have the capacity to actually go bankrupt – and some of them do! As you go a step beyond municipal governments, you can see why investing in corporate bonds becomes even more risky.

At the end of the day, never purchase a municipal or corporate bond without knowing the financial health of the issuer.
Methods for estimating this health are provided in the stock
valuation portion of this book. As you learn the techniques to
estimate the financial health of a company, you'll want to focus
on the debt to equity of a business and its continued earnings
potential.

* * *

Bond Math

As you probably already know, the yield of a bond is directly related to the length of borrowing. If you purchased a
bond for 30 years, you should expect a higher yield on your
money compared to a bond that matures in only a year. As you
look at the chart below, you'll see a generic representation of
this idea. Try to figure out how much interest you could expect
from a 15-year bond.

Bond yield curve (year XX01): Figure 6.1

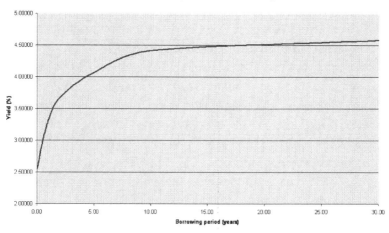

If you answered about 4.5%, you'd be right. As you look at this chart more closely, you'll notice some interesting things. As you assess the value of a 10-year bond versus a 30-year bond, you'll notice that the lender (or bond purchaser) isn't receiving a lot more interest for having his money tied up for an extra 20 years. Now, let's look at that same chart but at a different point in time.

Bond yield curve (year XX05): Figure 6.2

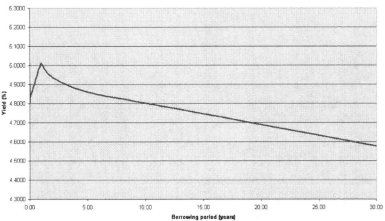

As you look at this chart, you'll notice the graph trends in a different direction. Before reading further, I want you to intuitively think about where the stock market might currently be at. Is it in a bull market or a bear market?

If you answered bull market, you're probably correct. In this scenario, you could expect analysts to estimate the average bond value over a 30-year period to be lower than the "bubble" rates. In this case, the short-term bonds are selling for 4.8% to 5% while the long-term bonds are down to 4.6%. As an investor, when you really begin to study yield curves, you'll begin to realize the importance they play: they're a great tool to generally determine over - and under - valued markets.

As a general rule of thumb, the average 30 year federal bond yields 5.4%.

The valuation of a bond is nothing more than three elements. First, how much money will I receive from all my coupons? Second, how much on average can I reinvest the coupons for? Third, how much money will I receive for the difference between my purchase price and the par value?

So, here are the important terms you must understand:

Par Value: This is the amount of money you'll receive when the bond is mature.

Term: This is the length of time the bond will last until par value is repaid to the owner of the security.

Coupon: This is the fixed annual payment an owner will receive until the maturity date.

Market Price: This is the price you can currently purchase the bond for.

Before continuing, I recommend getting a piece of paper, a pencil, a computer, and a calculator in order to practice the math that's about to be taught.

So let's take a look at how we would value a 10-year federal note that was just issued for $1,000 par and pays a 5% coupon. Assuming you purchased the note for exactly $1,000 on the first day it was issued, you could expect a $25 coupon payment every 6 months. If you were to simply collect your coupon payments and not reinvest the money, this table would represent the payments you would receive.

Date	Coupon	Total	Date	Coupon	Total
Jan-10	$25	$25	Jan-15	$25	$275
Jul-10	$25	$50	Jul-15	$25	$300
Jan-11	$25	$75	Jan-16	$25	$325
Jul-11	$25	$100	Jul-16	$25	$350
Jan-12	$25	$125	Jan-17	$25	$375
Jul-12	$25	$150	Jul-17	$25	$400
Jan-13	$25	$175	Jan-18	$25	$425
Jul-13	$25	$200	Jul-18	$25	$450
Jan-14	$25	$225	Jan-19	$25	$475
Jul-14	$25	$250	Jul-19	$25	$500

In addition to the $500 you would collect over a 10-year period, you would also receive the par value of $1,000 when the bond matures. So on July 2019, your $1,000 investment would now be worth $1,500.

As we look at the table above, we know there's a little piece of the puzzle missing. One of the things we aren't accounting for is the interest that will be paid on the coupon payments we receive every six months. This is where the valuation of the bond gets a little tricky. If you simply put the coupon payment into a checking account, the valuation is simple – you'll make $500 in 10 years on your investment. But if you take each coupon and reinvest the money, some guesswork and estimations need to take place on the overall value of this investment. Since there is no way of knowing how much interest you can get on your money each time you collect a coupon, you would need to estimate the average interest you could get over the 10-year period.

So where can you estimate the average interest rate for the next 10 years? Remember the yield curves? By simply looking at the current federal bond yield curve, you can estimate this number. Let's use Figure 6.2 as an example. As you look back at the 10-year interest rate on the curve, what did you find? If you answered 4.8%, you would be exactly right.

Now, how would our bond investment look if the coupon payments were reinvested at the 4.8% rate? Here's the new chart:

Date	Coupon	Total		Date	Coupon	Total
Jan-10	$25	$25		Jan-15	$25	$310
Jul-10	$25	$51		Jul-15	$25	$343
Jan-11	$25	$77		Jan-16	$25	$376
Jul-11	$25	$104		Jul-16	$25	$410
Jan-12	$25	$131		Jan-17	$25	$445
Jul-12	$25	$159		Jul-17	$25	$481
Jan-13	$25	$188		Jan-18	$25	$517
Jul-13	$25	$218		Jul-18	$25	$555
Jan-14	$25	$248		Jan-19	$25	$593
Jul-14	$25	$279		Jul-19	$25	$632

Although I solved this problem using code in Microsoft Excel, you may not have the programming skills necessary to solve this problem. In fact, much of the math that's associated with solving bond values is fairly complex and difficult to understand. Thankfully, there are calculators online that automatically solve these problems for us. For example, if you wanted to solve the above problem, you could simply input the following information at www.moneychimp.com.

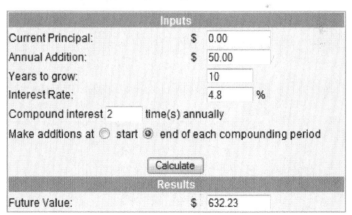

So where's all this math taking us? The answer is simple: the math will ultimately compare the value of competing assets. When we make this relative comparison (whether it's stocks or bonds), we need to know the future value of the money. In the above scenario, we found that a $1,000 bond would turn into

$1,632 if we held it for 10 years. But what would happen to the intrinsic value of that bond if interest rates drop to 4%? To solve this difficult but important problem, let's assume it's 2 years later and 8 years still remain on the bond's maturity.

Instead of going through the complicated math surrounding this problem, I'd like to direct your attention to an online bond calculator I've provided at www.BuffettsBooks.com. Under the Course 2, Unit 3, Lesson 3 learning module, you'll find the calculator you see below. The web address for this page is:

http://www.buffettsbooks.com/intelligent-investor/bonds/bond-calculator.html

If you get lost during any of the calculations, be sure to check out the video on the lesson page because it will show you how to use the calculator.

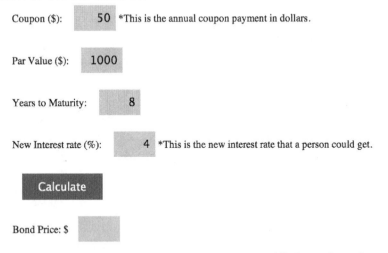

Coupon ($):   50   *This is the annual coupon payment in dollars.

Par Value ($):   1000

Years to Maturity: 8

New Interest rate (%):   4   *This is the new interest rate that a person could get.

Calculate

Bond Price: $

As you look at the following inputs, I'll describe why I used the following numbers for the scenario.

For the coupon, you'll need to enter the annual coupon payments. Since the note we initially purchased pays a 5% coupon, we know that we'll receive $50 a year for a $1,000 note.

Therefore, you'll enter 50 in the first blank box. Please note that this calculator only compounds the payments annually. Since the scenario was for biannual payments, the real answer would vary slightly. If you were doing this for a very large sum of bonds, you would want to use a more advanced calculator that accounts for bi-annual coupon payments. But for demonstration purposes, this calculator will get you very close to the right answer.

- For the par value, we simply enter 1000.
- The years to maturity is 8 years remaining.
- The new interest rate that we are comparing the bond to is a newly issued 4% federal note. Therefore, we enter 4 in the box labeled new interest rate.
- Once you complete these inputs, click on the "calculate" button in order to determine the market price.
- As you can see, the value of the bond increased to $1,067 after 2 years.

Something very important to consider is how the value of the bond changes with respect to the length of time remaining until maturity. For example, if our 10-year note would mature in only a year, the change in value would be much less; the price would only change to $1,009. If you would like to try this on the calculator, simply change the years to maturity to 1, then press the "calculate" button again. You can see, the more years that are left until a security matures, the more volatile the market price will be with interest rates. If this scenario were 28 years remaining and a 1% interest rate drop (or 100 basis point – that's a fancy way to say 1%), the value would have increased to $1,166.

Some might find it scary to purchase a long-term bond because of the volatility, whereas I see it as an enormous opportunity. When purchasing a bond at a high interest rate, I can't wait for the day to sell the bond when interest rates crash. The great thing about this strategy is while you are waiting for the interest rates to significantly decrease, you're collecting the coupon payments for owning the bond (which are high rates). By purchasing a long-term bond, you allow yourself enough time to experience the interest rate drop. When it happens, you get paid a great premium for owning the bond, and then you'll have cash in hand to purchase really cheap and valuable stocks.

* * *

Before concluding, I need to explain a few points before you begin your own research.

Callable or Redeemable Bonds: Since a bond is the same thing as a loan, your immediate thought should be concern over the callability of the asset. In a recession, when interest rates drop, homeowners choose to refinance their home. Homeowners compare the new closing costs with interest rates offered by banks in order to determine the financial gain of refinancing their home. Just like a homeowner, municipal governments and corporations want to do the same thing with their bonds. Instead of paying 6% interest, they choose to pay off their bonds and issue new securities at a much lower interest rate. Imagine experiencing the impact of this scenario if you just paid an enormous premium on a callable bond. Although the market price would never be this high for a callable bond, it's important to understand the callability before diving into municipal and corporate bonds. In most cases, federal bonds are not callable.

Non-federal Bonds: In this very brief chapter, I haven't even begun to discuss the value of corporate or municipal bonds. In order to properly value these assets, you need to take a cautious and methodical approach. The most important thing to understand is that non-federal bonds have the ability to fail. This means the company could go bankrupt and you could lose all your money. Although this is rare (especially for high-quality bonds), it's still a possibility. As you conduct more research on bond investing, you'll become familiar with a bond's rating. This rating does a cursory job of accounting for the risk associated with the company's or municipality's ability to repay the debt. Here are the different ratings:

Moody's		S&P		Fitch		
Long-term	Short-term	Long-term	Short-term	Long-term	Short-term	
Aaa		AAA		AAA		Prime
Aa1		AA+	A-1+	AA+	F1+	High-grade
Aa2	P-1	AA		AA		
Aa3		AA-		AA-		
A1		A+	A-1	A+	F1	Upper-medium-grade
A2		A		A		
A3	P-2	A-	A-2	A-	F2	
Baa1		BBB+		BBB+		
Baa2	P-3	BBB	A-3	BBB	F3	Lower-medium-grade
Baa3		BBB-		BBB-		
Ba1		BB+		BB+		Non-investment-grade speculative
Ba2		BB		BB		
Ba3		BB-	B	BB-	B	
B1		B+		B+		
B2		B		B		Highly speculative
B3		B-		B-		
Caa1	Not prime	CCC+				Substantial risks
Caa2		CCC				Extremely speculative
Caa3		CCC-	C	CCC	C	In default with little prospect for recovery
Ca		CC				
		C				
C				DDD		
/		D	/	DD	/	In default
/				D		

As you look at this chart, I highly encourage you to stay away from individual bonds in the non-investment-grade/ speculative category. In Security Analysis, Benjamin Graham spends an enormous amount of time describing techniques for valuing corporate and municipal bonds. From an individual investor's standpoint, the amount of risk associated with stepping into non-investment-grade bonds is beyond my appetite for risk.

Bond Indexes: A great way to invest in bonds is through a bond index. As you conduct research on this type of investment, you'll find a bond index trades on the market like a stock. Since the index pays a dividend (or modified coupon), you'll still receive money like a typical bond investment. One of the great things about an index is you can invest in lower-grade securities while limiting your risk due to diversification. How far you're willing to go is something you'll need to determine for yourself. For investors who lack the initial $1,000 or more to buy an individual bond, this provides a great opportunity. One of the disadvantages with a bond index is you won't see much of a price change with interest rates. This is due to the number of bonds and the varying length of maturities found in the index. If you invest in a bond index, I would never expect to receive more returns than the dividend/coupon that it pays quarterly.

As you look through this very basic chapter, it is the first step in understanding how these investments work. Although the basics are simple, there are numerous types of bonds that perform in all kinds of manners. For example, there are tax-free municipal bonds, corporate bonds, couponless bonds, inflation-proof bonds, and much, much more. All these different types of bonds have advantages and disadvantages – all which you need to understand.

The importance of this chapter is to teach you how to value the approach. During times of greed, when people are making enormous amounts of money in the stock market, you need to be thinking the opposite. You need to be potentially purchasing an armory of bonds, all yielding a nice coupon (probably above 4-5%), preparing for the financial storm that's bound to happen. It's only a matter of time before the stock market bubble will pop. When it does, you'll be prepared with your fixed-income bonds, ready to feed the appetite of the fearful. You'll then have the opportunity to sell those bonds (as long as they aren't callable) for substantial premiums.

Although Benjamin Graham's book, *Security Analysis*, discusses bond investing very well, I've also found The Bond Book, written by Annette Thau, to be outstanding. I highly encourage you to read this book and become familiar with all the different types of bonds that are available.

If you would like to watch the four video lessons that accompany this chapter on www.BuffettsBooks.com, simply navigate to course 2, unit 2.

Chapter 7
Valuing a Stock

In order to value a stock, a similar approach to the way we valued bonds is used. The main difference is an increased amount of caution and the number of variables. At first, the approach may be overwhelming. In order to grasp the concepts that are taught in this section, you'll need to try the techniques on your own. When you get lost or confused, start at the beginning of this chapter and slowly repeat the steps until it becomes comfortable. Since the math progressively builds upon itself, it's important to never skip a section you don't understand.

There are four rules to purchasing a company (or stock). All rules must be met. You cannot comply with some and disregard the others.

1. A stock must be managed by vigilant leaders.
2. A stock must have long-term prospects.
3. A stock must be stable and understandable.
4. A stock must be undervalued.

One of the things Warren Buffett is on the record for saying is that he always calculates the intrinsic value of a company before he looks at the trading price. He does this because he doesn't want to be influenced by the masses on the true value of any pick. I want you to keep this method in mind as you learn the following techniques.

Section 1
A stock must be managed by vigilant leaders.

Determining a leader's ethical behavior is often a very difficult task. Regardless of a leader's previous performance, some still commit heinous ethical acts and display poor behavior. As a small investor, you'll almost never have contact with the management of a business. With the advent of information online, I strongly encourage investors to research the CEO and board of directors for any stock pick they potentially want to invest in. Looking at the amount of money the CEO gets paid may relate to the ethical standards he places between himself and his employees. This will require you to do your own homework and determine what you consider desirable aspects of a leader. Here is a starting point for things to consider:

- A CEO who puts the interests of his employees before himself (through employee benefits and such)
- The composition of the board of directors
- A CEO who has a track record of conducting ethical business
- A CEO who doesn't get paid outrageous compensations

As you read through this list, it's obvious that a lot of these things are difficult to determine. You might be thinking that a business is much more than it's CEO – and it is. With that said, the direction of any organization starts at the top. The behavior is slowly adopted throughout the ranks like blood flowing from the heart.

Beyond the ethics, which are hard to determine, we can try and find vigilant leadership. Vigilant leadership is management that's always on the lookout for possible danger. Since danger to a company is financial ruin, we are looking for a company that has a track record for managing their debt flawlessly. If a company even possesses a hint of mismanaged debt, I'll immediately stop considering the pick (regardless of the Wall Street forecasts).

For me, there are too many great companies on the market with zero debt compared to businesses with similar products that carry a lot of leverage. I'm sure you've seen friends who take on a lot of debt in order to potentially get ahead of the pack. This is potentially fine for small businesses, but when you're dealing with billion-dollar corporations, debt makes the cards crumble during a recession. Think of debt as an instrument to accelerate time. Since intelligent investors aren't interested in getting to the finish line tomorrow, you shouldn't like the risk that debt imposes on your future rewards and hard-earned money. As you become more comfortable with investing, you'll find some sectors inherently carry more debt than others. For example, the financial industry carries more debt than a retailer. The amount of debt that you are comfortable with is something you'll need to refine as you continue to invest. Here are a few metrics I use in order to evaluate a business's control of debt.

Debt/Equity Ratio: This is called the debt-to-equity ratio. There are different forms of this ratio, but the primary version you need to understand is total debt divided by the company's equity. As you'll learn in the next section, "equity" is a very important term to understand. Equity is essentially what the company is worth – right now – if it sold everything and paid all its bills. The Debt/Equity ratio simply takes all the company's debt and divides it by that equity number. As you can quickly see, a low Debt/Equity ratio is a good thing. In fact, you'll find many companies that have a Debt/Equity ratio of zero. At the same time, you'll find numerous companies that have a Debt/Equity ratio of 5 or higher. For a company that has a Debt/Equity ratio of 5, that means it's got 5 times more debt than it has equity in the business. For me, that's a scary amount of debt and not something I want to take a chance on. There are plenty of businesses that carry no debt that have just as good of earnings as companies that carry large debt loads. (As a general rule of thumb, I try to always buy companies that have a Debt/ Equity ratio below 0.50)

Current Ratio: This ratio is a comparison of the current assets divided by the current liabilities. I find this ratio very important because it tells me if the business will need to take on debt in the next twelve months. When you learn about the balance sheet in the next section, you'll understand that a company reports its assets and liabilities every quarter for tax purposes. The sheet is broken down into long-term assets and liabilities and short-term assets and liabilities. In order for something to be listed as a short-term asset or liability, the company must anticipate receiving funds or paying funds within a twelve-month period. This provides a very good glimpse into the company's short-term outlook for the business. By dividing the short-term assets by the short-term liabilities, we'll quickly be able to determine if the company will be able to pay its bills for the next twelve months. Here is the equation for the current ratio:

Current Ratio = Current Assets / Current Liabilities

As you put hypothetical numbers into this equation, you'll quickly see that a 1.0 means the company won't owe or earn capital. As the number becomes larger, it becomes evident that the company has an easier time paying its liabilities and won't need to issue more debt. When I'm analyzing a business, I'll never consider a business that has a current ratio below a 1.0.

A third way to evaluate a company's fiscal responsibility is to review the rating on its bonds. As you learned in chapter 6, bonds typically have ratings from one of the three major rating agencies. These agencies rate the bonds based on the company's ability to repay the debt. Just like you have a credit score, companies receive similar scores on the bonds. A great way to quickly look at a company's financial health is to examine the rating on the bonds it's issued. You can find this rating on a lot of company websites under the investor relations tab. Although this is a quick and easy way to estimate the health, I still prefer to look at the D/E and current ratio first.

Although these are only a few techniques for measuring a business's acceptable leadership and debt levels, they are important characteristics to understand. Since we've already determined that we want to own a business for as long as possible, it should come as no surprise that a business that maintains low levels of debt will weather bad economies well; poorly managed debt will result in enormous market swings and years of slow growth during and following recessions. This principle will always serve you well during good times and bad.

If you would like to watch a video lesson that accompanies this rule on www.BuffettsBooks.com, simply navigate to course 2, unit 3, lesson 2.

Section 2
A stock must have long-term prospects.

One of the most fundamental concepts of making money in the stock market is buying a company that you can hold forever. This might sound completely counterintuitive to contemporary day traders, but for any investor who understands the time value of money, unrealized gains, and capital gains tax, holding your picks is essential.

The first reason for picking a long-time winner is obvious. You don't want your business to eventually turn sour. Predicting the viability of a business 10, 20, and even 30 years into the future is a difficult task. Although it might seem hard at first, let's list some products. As you look at each product, I want you to determine if each item will still be used in the year 2042.

Candy   Y or N
Hairspray   Y or N
iPod   Y or N
Steel   Y or N
DVDs   Y or N
Plastic   Y or N
Clothes   Y or N
Insurance   Y or N

As you look at the list, I'm sure some of the products will make you laugh as you think about their viability in 2042. At the same time, I'm sure a lot of the products will still exist in your perceived future world. In the end, you don't need a crystal ball to predict the direction of certain markets. Anyone's intuition can predict stable and unstable products for the future. When you look at the iPod, it should come as no surprise that in 2042, the existence of the iPod you know today will absolutely not be the same product then. Although Apple may be the leader in whatever emerging technology replaces the iPod, there is also a good chance it will not.

When you consider purchasing a business that deals with clothes, you might imagine the product still being viable in 2042, but will the business still be trendy? For example, if you were to invest in American Eagle, would its products still be the trend for children in 2042. I would argue that's a risky call. That doesn't mean it's not a great business, it just means it's something you need to be willing to accept the risk for.

The importance of finding a company that will produce stable returns forever is a smart investor's effort in avoiding taxes.

Every time a person trades a stock that has made money, he or she pays a portion of the gain to the federal government. This payment is made through capital gains tax. The amount owed in capital gains depends on the type of investment that was made and the duration it took to make the money.

For example, if you purchased a stock for $20 and sold it for $40 the next day, you would be taxed on your $20 gain at your ordinary income tax rate (for most people that is 25% to 30%). Therefore, if you are in a 25% tax bracket, you would immediately loose $5 of the $20 you just gained. This rule applies because this example is for a short-term capital gain. If you hold an investment for more than a year, you'll pay a 15% tax on your gain. To demonstrate the acidity of capital gains tax, focus your attention on the two charts below. The chart on the left is a $10,000 investment that compounds annually at 10%. The chart on the right is the same investment of $10,000, compounded at the same annual rate, but it accounts for a sale at the end of each year. As a result, the chart on the right pays a capital gains tax (25%) before the end of each year.

	Investment (10%)	Investment (10%)+tax
year 1	$10,000	$10,000
year 2	$11,000	$10,750
year 3	$12,100	$11,556
year 4	$13,310	$12,423
year 5	$14,641	$13,355
year 6	$16,105	$14,356
year 7	$17,716	$15,433
year 8	$19,487	$16,590
year 9	$21,436	$17,835
year 10	$23,579	$19,172
year 11	$25,937	$20,610
year 12	$28,531	$22,156
year 13	$31,384	$23,818
year 14	$34,523	$25,604
year 15	$37,975	$27,524
year 16	$41,772	$29,589
year 17	$45,950	$31,808
year 18	$50,545	$34,194
year 19	$55,599	$36,758
year 20	$61,159	$39,515

As you can see, in 20 years, the difference between the two investment approaches amounts to $21,644. This concept is called unrealized gains. When a person like Warren Buffett touts that he pays less taxes than his employees, this is how he does it. When he purchases stocks, he plans on owning the companies longer than his lifetime. As a result, he never pays capital gains on the stock's equity growth (which materializes through the growing market value). The only time you pay capital gains is when you sell the stock. (Please note that you will still pay taxes on dividends regardless of the length of ownership.) Understanding this important rule is the difference between amateur investors and intelligent investors.

If you would like to watch a video lesson that accompanies this rule on www.BuffettsBooks.com, simply navigate to course 2, unit 3, lesson 3.

Section 3
A stock must be stable and understandable.

One of the most basic tenants in valuing stocks is stability. Consider the following non-stock example.

Suppose you knew a high school student who had the following test scores over the past eleven years:

Andrew's test scores:

	Math	Science	English
1 Grade	A	A	A
2 Grade	A	A	B
3 Grade	A	A	A
4 Grade	B	A	A
5 Grade	A	A	A
6 Grade	A	A	A
7 Grade	A	A	A
8 Grade	A	B	A
9 Grade	A	A	A
10 Grade	A	A	A
11 Grade	A	A	A
12 Grade	?	?	?

Based on Andrew's past performance, what do you suppose he might receive in each subject for his 12th-grade year?

Let's conduct a similar experiment with a different student – Mike.

Mike's test scores:

	Math	Science	English
1 Grade	C	B	C
2 Grade	A	C	B
3 Grade	D	B	B
4 Grade	B	B	C
5 Grade	F	C	D
6 Grade	C	C	B
7 Grade	A	B	C
8 Grade	B	C	C
9 Grade	C	C	D
10 Grade	B	D	C
11 Grade	A	C	B
12 Grade	?	?	?

Based on Mike's past performance, what do you suppose he might receive in each subject for his 12th-grade year?

As we look at the two students, whose grades would be easier to predict? If you answered Andrew, I would completely agree. As we look at Mike's grades, I think we can conclude that his final grades would be difficult to predict because his past performance was volatile.

Taking this same principle and applying it to business, we can draw very similar conclusions. Right now, on the stock market, there are companies like Andrew and companies like Mike. As we look to invest in different businesses, you'll find a lot of investors are attracted to companies like Mike: companies that are volatile.

Now, that might seem counterintuitive considering a company with volatility is hard to predict. As you think about this concept, you must also understand that most investors lack patience. As a result, they are attracted to a company that could quickly change in value and put money in their pocket.

It is my opinion that the only proven way of making money in the stock market is a value-based approach – one in which an investor looks at a predictable company (with respect to past performance) and assesses its intrinsic value. This investor then compares the intrinsic value to the market price and makes a determination of whether the company is worth investing in. Without being able to predict reasonable performance into the future, calculating this value is impossible. At the end of the valuation portion of this chapter, I'll provide current examples of companies that have stable and unstable performance. As you become more involved in calculating these values, you'll quickly realize the importance of picking companies that possess stability.

Although I didn't provide examples on how to identify financial figures that demonstrate a stocks stability, the video tutorial that accompanies this lesson at www.buffettsbooks.com does. To watch the video on how to identify key financial terms that represent a stock's stability, simply navigate to course 2, unit 3, lesson 4.

Section 4
A stock that is severely undervalued.

So this is the part you've been waiting to read. How do I calculate the intrinsic value of a stock? Hang on tight, here comes the math.

In 1999, Warren Buffett wrote the following about intrinsic value:

"Intrinsic value can be defined simply: It is the discounted value of the cash that can be taken out of a business during its remaining life." –Warren Buffett

After reading this section, you'll be taught the tools that will allow you to look at a stock pick and estimate its current intrinsic value (i.e., it's worth $50 a share). In addition to estimating its value, you'll also be able to estimate its annual return. (i.e., my stock that's worth $50 a share should increase in value by 8% a year).

Before starting, here is Warren Buffett's reason for not sharing his calculations:

"The calculation of intrinsic value…is not so simple. As our definition suggests, intrinsic value is an estimate rather than a precise figure, and it is additionally an estimate that must be changed if interest rates move or forecasts of future cash flows are revised. Two people looking at the same set of facts…will almost inevitably come up with at least slightly different intrinsic value figures. That is one reason we never give you our estimates of intrinsic value." – Warren Buffett

Please keep this quote in mind as you learn the following techniques. Your appetite for risk and the movement of the federal note will have an enormous impact on the "estimated" intrinsic value.

Without delaying any more, I'll start by teaching the method for estimating the future cash flows of a business.

1
Estimating the future cash flows of a business

The estimated future cash flows of a company is calculated by estimating it's future book value (in ten years) and summing the company's dividend payments over the next ten years. We are only going ten years into the future because we'll then discount that cash flow by the current ten year federal note interest rate.

Future Cash Flows (ten year period) = Book Value Growth + Dividend Payments

For my readers who focus on earnings (because earnings are really important), please realize that book value (or equity per share) growth and dividends are the result of earnings. Below is a diagram that depicts the flow of money through a business. Start in the top left corner with the earnings of the business. (This will be discussed more in the next section, but earnings is the money remaining after all the employees, materials, and cost of making money is paid – it's the profit the business made for the year.)

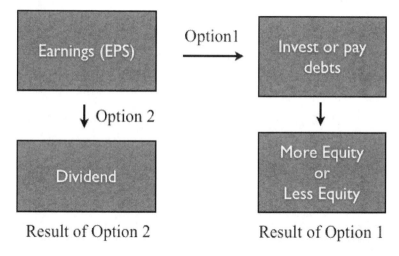

As you can see, a business has two options for handling its earnings. A company can invest the money back into the business or it can pay a dividend. As you look across the market, there are companies that do both options and there are companies that only focus on one. For example, a company like Facebook only takes option 1. Every dollar of earnings made is reinvested back into the company. Shareholders don't receive a dividend. As a result, the only way you'll make money owning Facebook is if the equity of the business continually increases. If the equity increases, the market will most likely value the trading price higher. As an intelligent investor, you'll want to find a company that does both. As you learn more, you'll quickly see that dividend payments help increase your overall cash flow and ability to continually reinvest in undervalued assets.

The important part here is to know that the expected return on a stock is based on dividends and equity growth. So let's learn about equity.

Equity

The best way I can explain equity to people is to provide an example of the definition in terms they can understand. To understand equity, I ask this simple question:

If you died today, how much money would you leave your family?

In order to figure out this number, you'll need to write down your assets and liabilities. Use the example on the next page to figure it out.

STOCK YOU

Assets

Short-term Assets

Current wages owed for work done this month	1,000	
Long-term Assets		
Ford F150	20,000	(this is the value if you sold it today)
Ford Mustang	15,000	
House	350,000	
Jewelry and such	5,000	
Furniture	5,000	(make sure you discount the value because it's used furniture)
TV	500	
Savings	75,000	
Checking	2,000	
Total Assets	**472,500**	

Liabilities

Short-term Liabilities

Current cable bill	12	
Current telephone bill	30	
Water bill	3	
Credit card debt	500	
Long-term Liabilities		
Ford F150	15,000	(this is the loan amount due today)
Ford Mustang	2,000	
House	200,000	
Total Liabilities	**217,500**	

Equity = *T.Assets - T.Liabilities*	**255,955**

Now, as we look at the number above, the equity is $255,955. This number is very important! In the above scenario, we can tell immediately whether the generic person mentioned is worth a dime or not. If this were a company's balance sheet, it would look very similar. In fact, I would challenge you to get online and pull up a company on MSN or Google and find its balance sheet. Be sure to look over the balance sheet in order to compare it to the example I provided above. As you look at that company's balance sheet, you would be able to tell the exact same thing: what this company would be worth if it ended its operations today. Believe it or not, there are numerous companies on the stock market, right now, that have negative equity.

In fact, in 2008, GM was worth less than $70 billion in negative equity! To my surprise, people still traded the company at $4 a share. Eventually, in 2009, GM went bankrupt and the shareholders lost all their money.

The point of this exercise is to allow you the opportunity to understand a very important term that is used in calculating the value of your future stock picks: equity. Just as you calculated your own equity, businesses do the exact same thing every quarter (or every three months). This calculation is done on a very important document called the balance sheet. You'll want to thoroughly understand this document if you want to trade stocks successfully.

The balance sheet is an important document because it shows the current equity of a business at a certain point in time. The question "If you died today..." applies to the company as well. If the company would liquidate (or sell everything and pay all its bills), the equity is what would be left. This equity is a starting point to understanding what the business is worth. In order to fully understand the balance sheet, I highly recommend buying a book that focuses completely on understanding corporate finance statements. I've provided recommendations at the end of this book. Also, if you go back to Course 1, Unit 1, Lesson 3, on the www.BuffettsBooks.com website, it gives a basic overview of a balance sheets.

Taking the concept of equity one step further, we can now talk about the term "book value." If you've ever been around a person who trades a lot of stock, you'll quickly hear "book value" being used. This term simply means equity per share. It's important to put everything in terms of one share because you want to always compare like terms. One of my pet peeves is when I hear a person talk in random terms. For example, I'll hear someone say "GM can't fail. It generates $30 billion in net income every year and its debt is only $9 a share."

When a person talks in unlike terms (meaning he uses figures that reference the business as a whole and then references the business as an individual stock), it immediately tells me he doesn't know what he's doing. In order for the numbers to make sense, you either need to consistently talk in terms of owning the entire business (which is a lot of billions and millions talk), or you need to consistently talk in per-share numbers. Obviously, the latter is easier and quicker.

In order to understand this concept with full clarity, think of stocks in a different light. Instead of looking at an individual share like an alien object, think of one share as the entire business. If it's easier to understand, imagine a mini business that you could fit in the palm of your hand. Since that "mini" business is so small, its equity isn't $30 million, it's $3. Once you make the leap to always comparing all the numbers in terms of a per-share figure, everything starts to make sense.

When someone says book value, he is really saying equity per share.

So, when we take the company's total equity and divide by the total number of shares outstanding, we get the book value (or equity per share).

Here's an example:

Total Equity / Total Shares Outstanding = Book Value

$255,955 / 10,000 = $25.60

(You'll notice I used the $255,000 in equity from the individual-person example used above. For the total shares outstanding, I simply "made up" a plausible number. For a real stock, you would simply look up the term, shares outstanding, and apply that number (the shares outstanding are reported at the bottom of the balance sheet). I then used the division to arrive at a book value of $25.60.)

As we look at the book value above, this number often serves as a reference point – a keystone, if you will. We know that if the company ended today (liquidated), it should be worth the amount of book value. In a simple world, people might think the company should trade on the stock market for the book value. This definitely is not the case. I'll explain more when I talk more about dividends and earnings.

Now let's try this for a real company. We'll use the large company Johnson & Johnson (JNJ) in order to calculate its book value. (Disclosure: I do not own shares of JNJ at the time of publication.)

First, we'll need to go to the company's balance sheet. Once you arrive at that page, you'll want to access its most recent quarterly report. (To see how this is done from Microsoft Money, flip to the back of the book to the section titled Common Stock Terms.) You'll notice that the numbers are reported in millions. Since the numbers are so big, the six zeros are dropped off of every number on the report. As you look at the report, you'll notice a very similar setup to the example we used above for the individual person. You'll see the equity is simply the difference between the total assets and total liabilities. You'll want to take that equity figure and divide it by the total number of shares outstanding (at the bottom of the balance sheet). Once you do that quick calculation, you should arrive at $20.95 (for the 4th quarter of 2011).

Book Value = Equity / Shares Outstanding

$20.95 a share = $57,080.0 / 2,724.36

If this isn't the number you found, or you're just having trouble calculating the book value, I highly encourage you not to move forward with the reading. This is something you really need to understand and know how to calculate. If this book isn't providing enough information for you to understand, I would start on the Internet to see if others have described the process in more comprehendible terms.

Now that you're an "expert" at calculating the book value, you'll want to focus your efforts on a very important assessment. One of the most important figures for an investor to understand is the consistency and amount of change associated with a company's book value. Let's look at the book value of Johnson & Johnson (JNJ) over the last nine years. If you want to learn how to find these numbers for a different company, flip to the back of the book and read the section titled Equity Growth in the Common Stock Terms Chapter.

Date - Book Value
01/12 - $20.95
01/11 - $20.66
01/10 - $18.37
12/08 - $15.35
12/07 - $15.25
12/06 - $13.59
01/06 - $13.01
01/05 - $10.71
12/03 - $9.05
12/02 - $7.65

As you look at the numbers above, you'll find they are relatively stable and predictable. You'll also notice that JNJ's book value (or equity per share) is growing almost every year. That is what you're looking for! If you plotted the numbers on a graph over time, it would look like this.

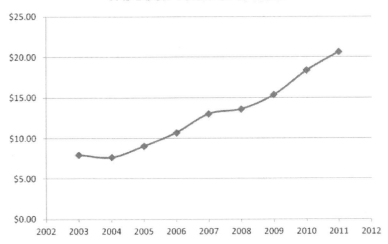

This chart serves as a great example of finding a company that has steady and calculable growth.

Warren Buffett's opinion on the growth of book value is fairly profound. Here's a direct quote from a piece he wrote on calculating intrinsic value:

"In other words, the percentage change in book value in any given year is likely to be reasonably close to that year's change in intrinsic value." –Warren Buffett

After looking at the annual book value (or equity per share) growth over a long period of time, it becomes very important to estimate what percent the book value is growing annually. Going back to the example where you calculated your own equity, we can all agree that it would be very important to know how your equity is changing from year to year. If, for instance, you wanted to know if you'd be a millionaire someday, tracking your personal equity growth from year to year would provide a very good indicator of your future value and ability to attain that goal. By tracking the rate at which your equity would change, you could predict the date you'd become a millionaire if your earnings remained constant. Evaluating the value of a business uses the same technique. If you look at the change in book value, you'll be able to quickly determine the direction and speed of growth associated with any business. When we look at the chart of JNJ's book value growth listed above, we essentially need to determine the slope of the line. When we determine that, we'll then have an estimate of how much the book value may grow from year-to-year into the future.

In order to calculate that number, we have two tools. The first tool can be found at www.BuffettsBooks.com. If you navigate to Course 2, Unit 3, Lesson 5, you'll find two calculators on that page. The first calculator provides a quick estimate for the average book value growth over any number of years you specify. In order to learn how to use the calculator, simply watch the video that's provided on the lesson page. In fact, the rest of the information you'll learn in this section is also provided in the video lesson. The second tool is a little more accurate, but requires more time to calculate.

If you'd like a weighted average book value growth, you'll want to execute the method below. Regardless of your decision (using the easy way or the hard way), if you're determining the growth for a stable company, both numbers will get you in the ballpark.

Average annual book value growth is calculated by the following:

$$\frac{(\text{Present Book Value - Previous Year's Book Value})}{\text{Previous Year's Book Value}} = \text{Annual Book Value Growth (\%)}$$

$$\frac{\$20.95 - \$20.66}{\$20.66} = 1.4\% \text{ (rounded)}$$

Now that we calculated the book value growth over a 1-year period, we need to conduct the same calculation for the remaining years in order to get a more predictable pattern of growth.

Year	Book Value	Book Value Growth Rate
01/12 - $20.95		1.4%
01/11 - $20.66		12.5%
01/10 - $18.37		19.7%
12/08 - $15.35		.66%
12/07 - $15.25		12.2%
12/06 - $13.59		4.5%
01/06 - $13.01		21.5%
01/05 - $10.71		18.3%
12/03 - $ 9.05		18.3%
12/02 - $ 7.65		

As we look at the numbers above, you'll realize that we only have 9 numbers for the book value growth rate. This is because we only have 10 data points. As a result, you'll have 1 less number – since the calculation takes the difference between years.

I like to find the difference between every year so I can see if the numbers are relatively consistent. If they aren't, I often try to understand why. For example, in 2008 there was an enormous economic recession. Therefore, 0.6% growth during that time makes sense.

NOTE: It is very important to always calculate this number using the book value and not the total equity found at the bottom of a balance sheet. By using the equity at the bottom of a balance sheet, you would fail to account for potential changes in the number of shares outstanding from year to year. In the end, it will give you false equity growth per share.

So, what do we do next?

Once I have these numbers, I simply find the average book value growth over the number of periods. Since I had 10 years of data and 9 periods of calculated growth, I'll average the percent change over 9 years.

$$\frac{\text{Sum of Book Value Growth}}{\text{Total Number of Figures}} = \text{Average Book Value Growth Over "n" Years}$$

$$\frac{(1.4 + 12.5 + 19.7 + .66 + 12.2 + 4.5 + 21.5 + 18.3 + 18.3)}{9} = 12.1\% \text{ over 9 years}$$

This is a significant number to understand. If you used the www.BuffettsBooks.com book value growth calculator (instead of the long-hand calculation above), you would have found the growth to be 11.8%. As you can see, the numbers are slightly different, but similar. Since we are using the numbers as an estimate for predicting future cash flows, either technique will work for a stable company.

Now don't forget, this company's book value is growing because of one figure – the earnings. As you look back to the beginning of this section, remember the diagram that shows the two options a company has to distribute or invest its earnings. If those earnings are decreasing, the book value growth and dividend payments can't be sustained at the previous rate. Always ensure the earnings will remain the same or increase in the near-term forecast. Almost any company you research will have a location where analysts predict the future earnings for the next year. If the earnings are decreasing, so will your book value growth and dividends. If you're conducting your research at www.money.msn.com, you can find the analyst's estimates for future earnings by clicking on the left-hand navigation bar under the tab titled "Earnings." In May 2012, the estimates for JNJ were, an EPS of $5.12 for 2012, and an EPS of $5.43 in 2013. As we look at those estimates, we can remain confident that

JNJ's growth will continue to move in the same direction as the earnings are consist with what we have seen in the past.

As I mentioned at the beginning of this chapter, the estimate for future cash flows is based on two significant figures: book value growth and dividends. Since we just estimated that the book value will grow at 12.1% annually, let's determine what the book value of JNJ will be in the year 2022. To calculate this problem, you'll simply use the following equation:

$$FV = PV \, (1+i)^n$$

FV = Future Book Value
PV = Present Book Value (or Current Book Value)
i = Book Value Growth Rate
n = Number of years into the future

Therefore when we substitute our terms, we get the following:

$$FV = \$20.95 \, (1 + .121)^{10}$$
$$FV = \$65.65$$

As you can see, it's very important to estimate the future book value because it will have an enormous impact on the future trading price. If the book value of JNJ was $65.65 today, it would obviously be trading much higher than its current $65 market price if earnings remained positive.

If the calculation above didn't make sense, don't worry. I have this automatically built into the calculator you'll find at the www.BuffettsBooks.com website. If you look at the second calculator found at the Course 2, Unit 3, Lesson 5 webpage, you'll notice that I prompt you for this information when calculating the overall intrinsic value.

Since the book value at the end of 2011 was worth $20.95 and we estimate that the book value in 2022 will be $65.65, our math predicts that one share of JNJ's book value will increase by $44.70 over the next ten years. This future book value figure is the first of two variables that are used in determining the sum of future cash flows. The second variable is the total dividend payments you'll receive over the next ten years. So let's learn about that now.

Dividends

The second part to determining the future cash flows is summing the expected dividend payments you'll receive over the next 10 years. When analyzing equity, we were assessing the company's change in book value over time. When assessing its dividends, we will be taking a closer look at a company's lifeblood, the earnings.

In order to calculate the earnings, you would start by looking at a company's income statement. The income statement is a form that businesses use in order to report the money it makes from the sale of its products and services. As mentioned earlier, the earnings are nothing more than the money that remains from the sales of the product and expenses paid to make money. Let's demonstrate the use of an income statement by first calculating your personal earnings. In order to make light of income statements, let's assume all your expenses are essential to your ability to produce revenue (that's the requirement for a business's income statement). I strongly recommend you calculate your own income statement using the example on the next page as a template. This will help you understand this concept.

Personal Income Statement (annual):

Revenues (money from employment)
Job pays (annual)   100,000

Total Revenues   100,000

Expenses (cost of living – or cost to produce revenue for a company)
Car payments	11,000	
House payment	24,000	
Food	6,000	
Internet and TV	1,200	
Phone	2,400	
Insurance	2,000	
Gas	7,400	
Luxuries	16,000	(these are things you spend money on that produce no equity, like vacations or going out to eat, etc.)
Total Expenses	70,000	(this number is also referred to as the cost of revenue)

Net Income   30,000 (Total Revenue - Total Expenses = Net Income)

As we look at this person's net income of $30,000, we can all agree this is a very profitable lifestyle. If the expenses exceeded the revenue – like it does in many households – debt must increase over time if the numbers remain constant. This is very important to understand.

Just like how we turned equity into a smaller and more desirable term – book value – we'll do the same thing with net income. Assuming the same division of shares as the equity scenario (10,000 shares), we'll now calculate the earnings per share (EPS).

$$\text{Earnings Per Share (EPS)} = \frac{\text{Net Income}}{\text{Total Number of Shares Outstanding}}$$

$$\text{EPS} = \$3.0 = \frac{\$30,000}{10,000}$$

During the equity scenario, we discovered the individual's book value was $25.60. Now we determined his EPS is $3.00 annually. So what does that mean?

It means this. If this was a business, it would do one of two things with the $3.00 of earnings per share: pay a portion of the earnings to the shareholder (known as a dividend) or retain the money as equity (therefore, the $25.60 of book value would increase). Like I said earlier, find a business that does both.

Remember, these are the options companies have to allocate their earnings:

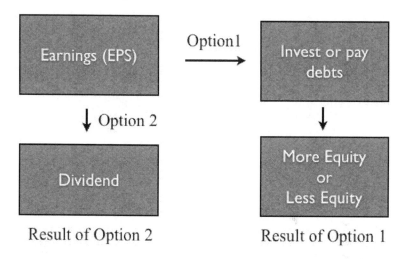

Result of Option 2   Result of Option 1

Now, let's look at how dividends are paid from the EPS for a real business. Since we were already looking at JNJ earlier, let's look at its numbers again.

On JNJ's income statement, look at the company's net income, found at the bottom of the income statement. Since the number is positive, it means JNJ's primary product (medicine) has produced a profit over the annual period. (Please note that I'm using the numbers from the annual income statement for the end of 2011. If you have different numbers, it's probably because you're looking at a different year.)

One of the advantages of working for a good company is the ability to get stock benefits. When a company offers stock benefits, it doesn't actually go through a financial broker and issue more shares. Instead, it keeps a list of shares that are owed to the employees over time. Depending on the deal that certain companies offer to employees, this may cost the business money. In order to account for this employee incentive, a term called "diluted earnings per share" is used. At the bottom of the income statement, you'll find a section that lists the diluted number of shares and also the diluted EPS. If you're really interested in getting precise numbers, you'll want to use the diluted values for all your calculations.

Here is the equation you should use to calculate the diluted EPS:

$$\text{Diluted Earnings Per Share (EPS)} = \frac{\text{Net Income}}{\text{Diluted Weighted Average Shares}}$$

$$\$3.49 \text{ per share} = \frac{\$9{,}672^*}{2{,}775.3^*}$$

*Note the numbers are in millions.

Now as we look at JNJ, a lot becomes clear. Here's a snapshot of the company at the end of 2011 with the essential numbers we've calculated so far:

JNJ Book Value: $20.95
JNJ's Average Equity Growth: 12.1% (average from 2003-2012)
JNJ's Diluted EPS: $3.49

Since the value of your stock will increase in value based on its equity growth and dividends, let's keep those figures in mind as we evaluate JNJ's dividend rate. If JNJ made $3.49 per share for the entire year, how could it pay a dividend higher than that amount without incurring debt? It can't (at least not for a long period of time), and as a smart investor, you'll need to always compare your dividend payment to the EPS or earnings generated by the company. In JNJ's case, it paid a $2.28

dividend in 2011 when its EPS was $3.49. This payment makes sense. It's not too much and it's not crumbs. If JNJ were paying a very small dividend, you better believe my expectation for equity growth would be very high.

As you can see, the magic number is the EPS: $3.49. That money is your earnings! Your business, or your one tiny share, made that $3.49 for the product(s) the company sold over the last year. As the owner of that one share, you're entitled to that money. That $3.49 doesn't go toward paying the employees or the CEO. Those expenses have already been paid before arriving at the final $3.49 figure. That money is yours! So how are you going to get that money in your pocket? Three ways:

Completely through dividends
or
Completely through book value growth
or
Both dividends and book value growth

Looking at JNJ, we see that the EPS diluted is $3.49. At the same time, when we see the company is paying a $2.28 dividend, we realize that dividend payment is 65% of the EPS. I find this number (the payout ratio) important because it quickly shows if a company is paying a "reasonable" dividend. Believe it or not, I see companies on the open market paying their owners dividends that exceed the EPS. It doesn't make sense, and I would strongly encourage you to avoid companies that slowly devour themselves in an effort to keep their shareholders happy. Typically, when I see a company making a "high" dividend payment (i.e., something that is 75% of its EPS), you'll typically notice that the company's book value (or equity per share) remains constant or even decreases in value from year to year.

The main reason I conduct this analysis is to determine whether the current dividend payment is sustainable. Once I've reached a conclusion whether it is or isn't, I'll then predict a conservative estimate of what future dividend payments might look like. For JNJ, I'd be comfortable estimating that the current dividend payment of $2.28 will continue for the next ten years. If you would like to make a more aggressive estimate, then use something higher. I typically like to use the current rate and if it changes in the future, then I'll just re-calculate the new intrinsic value. As you look at this objective method for estimating future cash flows, it becomes obvious why Warren Buffett has the following quote:

"The calculation of intrinsic value...is not so simple. As our definition suggests, intrinsic value is an estimate rather than a precise figure, and it is additionally an estimate that must be changed if interest rates move or forecasts of future cash flows are revised. Two people looking at the same set of facts...will almost inevitably come up with at least slightly different intrinsic value figures. That is one reason we never give you our estimates of intrinsic value." – Warren Buffett

So if we would sum the dividend payments over the next 10 years, we would have the following results:

2012 - $2.28
2013 - $2.28
2014 - $2.28
2015 - $2.28
2016 - $2.28
2017 - $2.28
2018 - $2.28
2029 - $2.28
2020 - $2.28
2021 - $2.28
Total = $22.80

*　*　*

In summary, we learned that the estimated future cash flow of a business is dependent on two figures:

Estimated future cash flows = Book Value Growth + Dividends

During our calculations, we estimated the following results for JNJ:

Average Book Value Growth per year = 12.1% Annually
Book Value at the beginning of 2022 = $65.65

Average Dividend Collected each year = $2.28 Annually
Total Dividends Collected by 2022 = $22.80

As we return to Warren Buffett's quote on how to calculate the intrinsic value of a company:

"Intrinsic value can be defined simply: It is the discounted value of the cash that can be taken out of a business during its remaining life." –Warren Buffett

You can see we have determined the second half of the quote – the cash that can be taken out of a business during its remaining life. For us, we have set the remaining life to 10 years because as we move into part 2, we'll now discount that cash flow by the 10 year federal note.

2
Current Intrinsic Value

In order to determine the intrinsic value of a company, we now need to discount the cash flow we determined above, back to the present day value. If you're really curious what math formula is used to discount the cash flow, it is listed below:

$$IV = Div \cdot \frac{\left[1 - \left[\dfrac{1}{(1+i)^n}\right]\right]}{i} + \frac{FBV}{(1+i)^n}$$

If that calculation makes your head hurt, simply use the intrinsic value calculator I've provided on the website. You can access the calculator by going to Course 2, Unit 3, Lesson 5, or simply click on the "calculator" quick link at the top of every page and select "Intrinsic Value (stocks)."

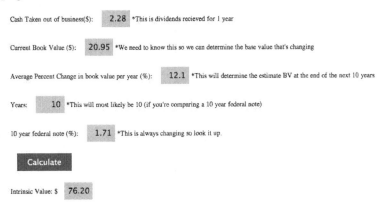

Cash Taken out of business($):   2.28   *This is dividends recieved for 1 year

Current Book Value ($):   20.95   *We need to know this so we can determine the base value that's changing

Average Percent Change in book value per year (%):   12.1   *This will determine the estimate BV at the end of the next 10 years

Years: 10   *This will most likely be 10 (if you're comparing a 10 year federal note)

10 year federal note (%):   1.71   *This is always changing so look it up.

Calculate

Intrinsic Value: $ 76.20

Here is a list of the variables that were input into the calculator:

1. Cash taken out of business ($) : this is simply the annual dividend you would expect to receive over the next ten years of owning this company. Make sure you only use the dividend for 1 year. The calculator automatically sums those dividend payments for the ten years.

2. Current Book Value ($) : This number is input into the calculator as a baseline value. It then uses the third input to estimate the book value in ten years.

3. Average percent change in book value per year (%) : This is the number you would have determined either in long-

hand or from the first calculator found on the webpage you're currently using.

4. Years : This is the number of years that you want the calculator to sum the dividend payments and estimated book value figure. Since we'll be discounting the cash flow from the ten year federal note, we'll use 10 here.

5. 10 year federal note (%) : This figure can be found at the following web address:

> *http://www.treasury.gov/resource-center/data-chart-center/interest-rates/Pages/TextView.aspx?data=yield.*

Please realize this number changes almost every day, so as you reassess the intrinsic value of a company, it will absolutely change with the movement of interest rates.

Note: Please ensure you don't use $ or % signs when providing your inputs to the calculator. Also note that you DO NOT enter percentages as .01 for 1%. The correct format for entering 1% into the calculator is simply 1.

So what does the intrinsic value of $76.20 mean?

It is our humble estimate that if you could buy JNJ for $76.20 (on the day I did this calculation), you could expect a 1.71% return on your investment over the next ten years.

Since JNJ is actually trading lower than $76.20 (it's trading for about $65.00 a share), you'll get a better return than the 10 year federal note (1.71%).

So you're next question is probably – How much better of a return?

Lucky for you, you can simply adjust the input of the 10 year federal return and find out for yourself. Although this method takes a little trial and error on the calculator, you can usually figure it out in a matter of seconds. In order to estimate the return you would receive based on the current market price, simply change the number found in the "10 year federal note (%)" input box until the intrinsic value equals the current market price. An example of this is provided at the end of the video found on the web page.

In order to get the intrinsic value to equal $65, I had to change the "10 year federal note (%)" from 1.71 to 3.59 (which means 3.59%).

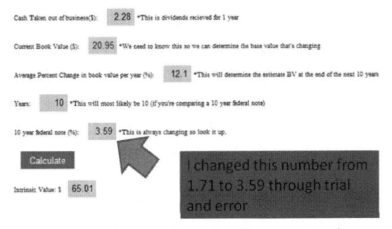

This means that if you buy JNJ at the current market price of $65 a share, it's estimated that a 3.59% return on your investment might occur over the next ten years.

Now for the big question!

Do you purchase a zero risk investment (the ten year federal note) and receive a 1.71% return for the next ten years?

Or...

Do you assume some risk and purchase JNJ and potentially receive a 3.59% return for the next ten years? So this is where your appetite for risk plays an enormous role in your decisions as an investor. Is double the return worth the risk of buying a stock that may or may not produce the cash flow we just estimated? This is where I can no longer help you. This risk is something that you'll have to determine for yourself. As for me, I wouldn't be satisfied with either one of these returns, so I'd be looking at another company or bond to invest in.

Regardless of the marginal returns, the method for determining the value is the important part I want you to learn.

If you've understood everything to this point, you're well on your way to cracking the code that Buffett uses for calculating intrinsic value. As you can see, the 10 year federal note is nothing more than a baseline value that we can use to relatively compare all investments. Think of it as a ruler. Without a ruler, people wouldn't have the ability to relatively compare the length of different objects. The ten year federal note is no different. If any of this information was confusing, I strongly encourage you to reread the chapter, watch the videos on the www.buffettsbooks.com website, and sign up for the forum I have on the website so you can ask your questions there. I'll be sure to help assist in any way I can.

Summary

Although JNJ is a very stable and predictable company that possesses very little debt, the multiple at which investors trade the company to its book is very high. Benjamin Graham would probably have a difficult time buying this company simply because of the margin of safety discussed earlier. Since the book value on the company is only $20.95, traders could potentially move the market price much lower if earnings began to slow. Benjamin Graham really tried to avoid buying companies that traded at a multiple higher than 1.5 times the book value. As you assess your tolerance for risk, always be mindful of this concern.

Something I really want to make clear is that my estimation that JNJ's intrinsic value is worth $76.20 is not concrete. This value is only true if the future cash flows are accurate. Also remember that the $76.20 value will only yield a 1.71% return. Regardless of whether that estimate is correct, we can relatively say with confidence that the company's book value has grown consistently and predictably. This is one of the reasons stability is so important when analyzing a company's potential to earn in the future. I want everyone to understand that this method should be used as a rule of thumb. In the end, this method should be used to estimate your annual stock growth and to determine whether you're buying the company at a reasonable price or an overvalued price.

You'll note my investment decisions are completely based on relative factors. Since the market is constantly changing, you'll need to conduct this assessment anytime you wish to purchase a security (stock, bond, or any type of investment). Prices are increasing or decreasing on a secondly basis – interest rates are doing the same. The important part isn't tracking the day-to-day changes. The important part is assessing the best-priced asset for any time you have cash to invest. Since balance sheets, income statements, and cash flow statements are updated quarterly, there is no point in worrying about the day-to-day trading that occurs on the market. Using these principles puts you in a different category of investing. Instead of playing the market like a professional Las Vegas gambler, you're now employed with the techniques of a patient and informed investor – like Warren Buffett or Benjamin Graham.

As you can see, these calculations mean absolutely nothing if the business isn't stable. Trying to calculate the value of an emerging business is a waste of my time and speculative. I like to use the following rule when assessing my investment versus speculation approach:

- Investing is when you don't know what could go wrong.
- Speculation is when you know exactly what could go wrong.

As a general rule of thumb, here are the key numbers that I like to use when looking for companies to invest in. Below is a screen capture from Google stock screener for the starting ratios I use to find companies. Depending on the current market conditions, the number of stocks the screener may find will vary. Your job is to change the slide rules for the amount of risk you're willing to assume for the certain categories. In order to try the stock screener, go to the following web address: *http://www.google.com/finance#stockscreener.*

Criteria	Min	Company Distribution	Max	
Market cap ⑦	100M		481.47B	☒
P/E ratio ⑦	0		15	☒
Div yield (%) ⑦	2		7	☒
Price to book ⑦	0		1.5	☒
Current ratio ⑦	1.5		5	☒
Total debt/equity (Recent qtr) (%) ⑦	0		1.2	☒
Return on equity (5 yr avg) (%) ⑦	7		42154	☒
Return on equity (Recent yr) (%) ⑦	7		31195	☒

A Demonstration of a Speculative Stock Pick

To demonstrate an important point on picking stable companies, I'm going to identify a popular stock pick at the time of publishing and demonstrate why it's difficult to value: Sirius XM Radio (SIRI).

In my humble opinion, SIRI is a speculative stock. I say that because the company has volatile numbers that are not only hard to predict, but I'd say impossible to predict. Although analysts may predict next year's earnings fairly well, I'd argue they have no clue what the earnings will look like in five years. This is where SIRI is completely different than JNJ. Johnson & Johnson has maintained steady, consistent, positive earnings for the last ten years. Its earnings and equity growth is stable and predictable. As a result, I'm fairly confident I'll be able to predict its earnings ten years from now.

I'm now going to conduct an abbreviated analysis of SIRI:

Book Value for the Last 10 Years		Debt/Equity
2011	$.13	6.12
2010	$.05	15.5
2009	$.02	32.21
2008	$.00	377.24
2007	$ -.54	-1.66
2006	$ -.27	-2.75
2005	$.24	3.34
2004	$.78	.66
2003	$1.16	.15
2002	$7.33	1.18
2001	$14.06	.81

As you look at the initial book value and debt, it becomes obvious that you're looking at a business that is very unstable and has experienced a lot of turbulence.

At the time of publishing, SIRI is selling for $2.31 a share. That number is 17.7 times the book value of the business. Since the book value's growth is all over the place, it's nearly impossible to predict the future direction of the company's equity.

Now let's look at the company's earnings. In 2011, the company's EPS is $.07. This means that for every share you purchase on the market for $2.31, you can expect the share to earn $.07 annually. From the $.07, you'll earn no dividend. The expected earnings for 2012 is $.09 per share annually.

Without going any further into the analysis, you can quickly see that the company's numbers don't even make logical sense. Why would a person possibly pay 17 times the book value for a business that only makes $.07 a year? The person who would invest in this business would try to make the argument that the earnings are growing, and as a result, they will be able to compensate for the enormous premium paid over the book. Although the earnings are increasing with the projected estimate, it's not nearly enough of a margin to substantiate paying 17 times the book value. As soon as companies like SIRI miss their earnings expectation, day traders quickly undersell the previous trading price and there goes your money.

Going back to the little saying:

- Investing is when you don't know what could go wrong.
- Speculation is when you know exactly what could go wrong.

Here, we know exactly what could go wrong. SIRI could miss an earnings call by a penny or two and the market price would plummet. In the end, could an individual make money by purchasing shares of SIRI? Absolutely. Does the investment display a conservative approach to investing hard-earned money? I don't think so.

Part II Summary

This guide is truly the tip of the iceberg. As you were reading this chapter, you were either completely confused or excited with the new investing approach. The more you understand corporate accounting, the quicker you'll be able to decipher the mathematical code that businesses report every quarter. As you can see, math plays an important part in understanding the value of a business. Without understanding these skills, I would strongly discourage anyone from value investing in individual stock picks.

PART III
The Other Important Stuff

A s I sit here at my computer editing the first two parts of this book, I find myself frustrated with the amount of information that is missing from the book. Understanding the art of investing that is described in Warren Buffett's three favorite books is a daunting task to say the least.

In this last portion of the book, I'm going to try and tie up the loose ends from the first two parts of the book. I purposely didn't mention these subjects in Part II because I wanted you to remain focused on the fundamentals. If you had difficulty understanding any of the content that has been presented up to this point, I strongly discourage you from reading further. The somewhat random points that will be discussed are very important but won't make sense unless a thorough understanding of the previous information is established.

If you ever have any questions or would like to get the opinions of other followers on the methods for valuing assets, I strongly encourage you to subscribe to the blog and forum found at the www.BuffettsBooks.com website. I love working with my readers and their interests, so don't hesitate to participate.

Chapter 8
Preferred Stock

Another great way to invest your money is through preferred shares. Although some might suspect that preferred shares are a lot like common shares, they might be surprised to know that preferred stock is more like bonds. If a company were to ever go out of business, a corporate liquidation would occur. This simply means the bondholders, preferred stockholders, and common stockholders would sell all the assets, pay all the liabilities, then split what's left. The tricky part becomes the order in which these investors get their fair share. Below is the order of precedence for a company bankruptcy:

1. Bond Holders
2. Preferred stock holders
3. Common Stock holders

During a corporate bankruptcy, a company would most likely have negative equity. As a result, the investors (listed above) would receive their portion of the assets in the order listed above. If the company had $100,000 in assets and $200,000 in debt, guess who gets all the assets? That's right, the bondholders. In that scenario, the preferred shareholders and the common shareholders would receive nothing.

Just like bonds, preferred shares are sold at a par value. For example, a preferred share may be issued for $100 par and it might pay a $9 dividend every year. Based on those numbers, 1 share is paying a 9% dividend to the owner. Although the preferred share may not have a maturity date, almost all preferred shares are callable. As a result, you may purchase a high-yielding preferred share, but it may be called. If this happens, you would most likely be paid back the par value plus 1 year's dividend. So for our generic scenario, you would be paid

$109 if this preferred share was called.

If owning a preferred share is something that interests you, you'll want to become more familiar with a document called an indenture. This is the document that specifies whether a preferred share is participating versus nonparticipating, cumulative versus noncumulative, callable, convertible, or a combination of all these features.

The important part to note is that a preferred share is valued just like a bond. If the company goes bankrupt, you'll be paid your par value after all bondholders are paid. As one might expect, preferred shareholders will always receive their dividends before common shareholders.

Shareholders' Equity with Preferred Shares

An important aspect that wasn't discussed in Part II of this book is how to account for the company's book value when a company has preferred shares. You'll absolutely want to ensure you understand how to do this calculation if you're investing in individual stock picks that also possess preferred shares.

To arrive at the total book value of the common stock, compute the total book value of the preferred stock, then subtract that amount from the total stockholders' equity.

Common Stockholders' Equity = Total Stockholders' Equity - Total Book Value of Preferred Stock

First you'll need to calculate the total book value of the preferred stock. In order to do this, find the book value of 1 share. This is done by finding the call price plus any dividends in arrears. If you have a noncumulative preferred stock, then it's simply the call price. Going back to our $100 preferred share, let's assume that the call price on the stock is $110. If the preferred share is noncumulative, then the book value is $110. If the stock is cumulative and the corporation owes 2 years of dividends, then the book value is $128. This was calcuated by taking the call price ($110) plus the 2 dividend payments ($9 each for a total of $18).

Let's assume that we used cummulative preferred share and the book value per share is $128. In order to find the total book value of preferred stock, we would simply take that $128 and multiply it by the total number of preferred shares. For simplicity, let's assume 1,000 preferred shares were issued. As a result, the total book value of preferred stock would be $128,000.

Now that we know that figure, we can subtract it from the total stockholders' equity to find the common shareholder's equity. Let's assume the total stockholders' equity on the balance sheet is $1,000,000 and there are 2,000 common shares outstanding. Based on those figures, let's solve for the common stockholders' equity and book value:

Common Stockholders' Equity = $1,000,000 - $128,000

Common Stockholders' Equity = $872,000

In order to calculate the common stockholders' book value, we would then divide by the 2,000 common shares outstanding:

$$\text{Common Shareholders' Book Value} = \frac{\text{Common Stockholders' Equity}}{\text{Common Shares Outstanding}}$$

Common Shareholders' Book Value = $872,000 / 2000 = $436

Now, all that math might seem really laborious, but as a common shareholder, it's important to understand how and why it's being done.

Preferred Shares Summary

Preferred shares are a great opportunity for investors to make investments that are less risky than common shares and better returns than bonds. As you might expect, the trading price of preferred shares really doesn't change very much. Like bonds, the market price will change based on financial health , maturity, callability, changing interest rates...etc. You'll definitely want to understand the company's ability to complete its dividends as a preferred shareholder. In the end, adopting a very similar approach to bonds will help you properly value preferred shares.

If you would like to watch the video lessons that give more insights and metrics for investing in preferred shares, be sure to navigate to course 2, unit 4 on the on www.BuffettsBooks.com website.

Chapter 9
Saving your Money and Cash Flow

According to a 2009 Sports Illustrated article, 78% of National Football League players are either bankrupt or in financial trouble within 2 years of retirement. An estimated 60% of National Basketball Association players are completely bankrupt within 5 years of their retirement.

Now you might be thinking How in the world is that possible?

The reason I started this chapter with those statistics isn't because I want to make professional athletes look stupid. I highlighted these points in order to emphasize the importance of savings and cash flow regardless of your annual income. For many people, they have the mindset that their next promotion or higher-paying salary will whisk away all their problems. Ironically, when these same people get a raise and make an additional $5,000 a year, they buy a new vehicle that raises their annual payments to $6,000 a year!

The problem most people have is the discipline to live within their means and stay there. For the poor professional athletes, they lived the high life and never did anything to turn their limited savings and massive cash flow into assets that would snowball their monthly income.

When you look at your personal financies, analyze what happens to your money each month. After you recieve all your salaries, dividend payments, coupon payments, royalties, etc., and pay all your bills, what do you have left? Now, the even more important question is how much of that money do you then use to invest in an asset that's going to put more money in your pocket the following month? If you said none, that's fine. That's why you're reading this book and learning how to fix your strategy.

This is important: You need to buy assets that will put

more money in your pocket every month.

By subscribing to the above guidance, you'll gradually build more cash flow and an ability to put your money into the most undervalued asset each month. This has a compounding effect.

So, how does that happen?

Simple. You need to figure out how much money you can afford to save (long term - like forever) each month without affecting your day-to-day life. For most people, when they start understanding the method for accumulating wealth, they're overaggressive. This is bad. You'll most likely exceed your ability to save long-term money and it'll result in you spending it all on a boat or a new car. When I say save it forever, I mean forever. You want new-car money, put it in a different savings account.

So let's assume you can put $500 into a long-term investment. Instead of looking at the market value of that investment as liquid cash, you need to view it as part of a company you can't afford to sell. You need to think like this: If I invest that $500 in a stock that pays a 4% dividend, I just increased my annual salary by $20 a year. That means I'll now have $501.60 to invest the very next month (since $20 / 12 months = $1.60 per month). Now this might not sound like much, but the compounding effect of this technique is profound. You'll also want to note that the share price of your stock picks will increase over time as well. But in this scenario, we are only talking about the dividend payments and their effect on increasing your cash flow. Increasing your cash flow every month is a key pillar to investing like Warren Buffett.

As you assess your cash flow, you'll quickly find that it's the lifeblood of your future lifestyle. If at the end of the month you have $500 to invest in assets, then you're probably better off than 60% of the professional athletes who make millions every year. For them, they are simply drinking all the water out of a 5-year well. As for you, your assets might be a lot smaller, but they are gradually becoming larger, and that well is never going to go dry.

One of the things Warren Buffett is most famous for is being frugal with his money. Now I'm not saying that's a good
thing, but I am saying you need to live within your means. If
you receive a pay raise, you need to be very methodical in how
much of the raise is going to be contributed toward buying new
assets each month. If you're going to spend money on a liability
(i.e., a new car), you want to be sure it's not disrupting your
ability to continually grow your assets.

If the stock market is overvalued, use your cash flow to
purchase high-yielding bonds. If the market just crashed and
stocks are selling cheap, use your cash flow to purchase the
undervalued stocks. Just remember, if you're not taking steps
to purchase new assets each month, you'll never improve your
current standard of living. Increasing your standard of living
through the use of debt is a mirage that leads you down a long
dry path. In the long run, you'll be thirstier than when you
started.

The Cash Flow Statement

Now that I've mentioned the importance of increasing
your personal cash flow, I'm going to talk about the cash flow
of a business. Every quarter when a company files its quarterly
tax report, it files a form called the cash flow statement. If you
haven't noticed yet, companies pretty much do the same thing
as people. The only reason most people don't understand corporate accounting is because they've never been taught and/or
never found it useful.

Since the income statement (used to find the EPS) is
prepared under the accrual basis of accounting, the revenues
reported may not have been actually collected. Similarly, the
expenses listed in the income statement may not have been
paid either. Now, some savvy investors can go back and inter-
pret the information from the balance sheet to figure out fact

from fiction, but there's no need with the advent of the cash flow statement. Back when Benjamin Graham wrote Security Analysis and The Intelligent Investor, cash flow statements weren't reporting requirements. Now they are.

If we were to personally track all the money that flows in and out of your bank accounts, how would we tackle that problem?

Well, we would look at your operating activities, your investing activities, and your financing activities. These are the three components of the cash flow statement (for a business).

- Operating Activities: This is all the activity that involves earning money.
- Investing Activities: This is all the activity that involves buying or selling assets.
- Financing Activities: This is all the activity that involves acquiring debt or paying it off.

Below is a generic cash flow statement for stock YOU:

Net income from job	$70,000
Net income from dividends	$500
Net income from coupons	$100
Cash from Operating Activities	$70,600
Investment in stocks	$-12,000
Investment in bonds	$- 4,000
Cash from Investing Activities	$-16,000
Retirement of car debt	$-6,000
Retirement of house debt	$-20,400
Cash from financing activities	$-26,400
Net Change in Cash	$28,200

Now, as we look at this rudimentary example of a personal cash flow statement, we can see that a net change in cash of $28,200 occurred for the annual period. Since this example is talking about an individual, we can assume that the $28,200 went to food and other miscellaneous expenses. The reason I use this example is to demonstrate the investing activities and financing activities in an understandable scenario. In both of the categories, you'll notice that the cash flow is negative. This means that $16,000 was used to buy stock and bonds. Under financing activities, it also meant that $26,400 was spent paying off debt. This is a good thing! If the cash flow statement had a positive sign for both of these activities, that would mean investments were sold and debt was incurred, respectively.

For a company like Johnson & Johnson, its cash flow statement looks like this (from msn money):

⦿ Annual ◯ Interim

	2011
Period End Date	01/01/2012
Period Length	12 Months
Stmt Source	10-K
Stmt Source Date	02/23/2012
Stmt Update Type	Updated
Net Income/Starting Line	9,672.0
Depreciation/Depletion	3,158.0
Amortization	0.0
Deferred Taxes	-836.0
▶ Non-Cash Items	653.0
▶ Changes in Working Capital	1,651.0
Cash from Operating Activities	**14,298.0**
▶ Capital Expenditures	-2,893.0
▶ Other Investing Cash Flow Items, Total	-1,719.0
Cash from Investing Activities	**-4,612.0**
▶ Financing Cash Flow Items	0.0
Total Cash Dividends Paid	-6,156.0
Issuance (Retirement) of Stock, Net	-1,279.0
Issuance (Retirement) of Debt, Net	2,983.0
Cash from Financing Activities	**-4,452.0**
Foreign Exchange Effects	-47.0
Net Change in Cash	**5,187.0**
Net Cash - Beginning Balance	19,355.0
Net Cash - Ending Balance	24,542.0

Financial data in USD
Values in Millions (Except for per share items)

As you look at the corporate cash flow statement, you'll notice that it's a little more complicated. Although it has more variables, the three fundamental elements should still jump out at you. As you look at the values, make sure you realize all the numbers have six zeros dropped off the end.

As we assess the cash from operating activity, we see the company had a positive cash flow of $14.3 billion (for the year 2011). From that $14.3 billion, it used $4.6 billion to invest and $4.5 billion to pay off debts. The remainder added $5.2 billion to the company's net cash on hand. If you wanted to figure out how much of that was on a per-share basis, simply divide by the number of shares outstanding (2.724 billion shares). It equals $1.90 per share.

So what does that mean?

Well, if it was your personal cash flow statement, what would it mean? That's right, you would probably have a lot of flexibility to do what you want. You would have the ability to invest more, you would have the ability to pay off more debt, and you would have the ability to put away cash for a rainy day. All these things are beneficial to a company, just like they are beneficial to you. A company that has a solid cash flow statement is a company that can make moves on markets that are undervalued. Most importantly, a company that has a growing cash flow statement is a company that'll continue to grow its equity and dividends.

As you look at all the numbers on the cash flow statement, realize that you'll need to conduct more research on your own in order to master its intricate fundamentals. The important part is understanding the basics.

If you would like to watch the video lessons that accompany this chapter on www.BuffettsBooks.com, simply navigate to course 2, unit 5.

Chapter 10
When Do I Sell?

Hopefully never! That's if you've picked a great company at a great price. I know this might sound completely counterintuitive, but the name of the game is really trying to find an asset that you never need to sell. To understand this idea of holding, look at your investments like a small business owner.

Let's say you just started your very own coffee shop on Main Street. As a new business owner, you hire your employees and sell your great product. After the first year, you are fortunate to have a successful new business. That's rare. You calculate your corporate year-end profit margin and realize that after paying all your employees and bills, the business made $30,000. Since the startup fees were $100,000, you quickly realize your investment returned 30%. With happy customers and a business model that shows promise for even more earnings next year, would you then decide to sell the business?

When you look at share ownership from this standpoint, it really becomes quite silly to think about selling shares of a business in only five days. As an intuitive person, I think you can agree that when shares are simply purchased and sold on emotions, it goes against sound judgment.

As you'll remember from Part II of this book, I talked about the concept of unrealized gains. This is the primary reason powerful investors like Buffett rarely sell their shares. In the end, they simply want to avoid paying taxes on the increasing value of their shares from year to year.

But in order to discuss this subject properly, we must be realistic and make the assumption that you'll eventually pick a company that you want or need to sell. If this is the case, the decision to sell needs to be strategic and not emotional.

Let's walk through a generic sell scenario to demonstrate

my point.

Let's assume you purchased 1,000 shares of company XXX at $50 a share. The book value on the company was $48 a share and you felt the intrinsic value was $70 a share when comparing it to a 3% ten year federal note and book value growth of 7% a year. Over the past 3 years, your company's market price actually increased to $70 a share. Although the value increased, your company's book value never increased and it's starting to show signs of mismanagement. Although you were right about the company's value, it has incurred a lot of debt and it doesn't look promising in the future. When you originally purchased the company, it carried a reasonable debt/equity ratio at 0.5. Then in the last 6 months, the company's leadership changed and you've noticed the company's debt/equity has increased to a 3.0. As the red flags in your mind start to rise, you do more homework on the drastic changes occurring inside your company. (Always tell yourself that it's your company. Think like an owner and you'll act like an owner.) After digging in the investor relations portion of the company website, you discover that earnings have drastically decreased and future earnings are grim at best. After a little math, you figure out that the equity in the company may only grow at about 5% a year, and its current intrinsic value is now $50 a share when compared to the newly issued 4.5% ten year federal note. Since the news doesn't sit well with your fundamental values, you look for a new company/asset to buy in place of company XXX.

After looking around the market, most stocks are actually trading at very high premiums. It appears you're now in a bull market, and the price to purchase a company isn't as attractive as 3 years earlier. After much searching, you come across a company called TTT and it seems to be a good buy. The company is trading for $50 and you estimate that its intrinsic value is $55 a share when compared to the 4.5% ten year federal note. By chance, this company's book value is also $48 a share, but you estimate that its book value is growing at 6% a year.

To simplify the scenario, let's assume both companies don't pay a dividend (in your real picks, make sure you're always buying dividend companies).

Now, based on those two companies, is it smarter for you to keep company XXX or sell the shares and buy the new attractive TTT?

Before I start to answer this question, I'll say that no one should hold-on to companies that have poor fundamentals and change their direction in a way you don't agree with. In fact, that's one of my top reasons for selling. In this situation, I would have sold company XXX because of the high debt levels. That fact aside, the second reason to sell is purely because the new company will produce better returns than the company you currently own. So in an effort to calculate that second reason, let's compare XXX and TTT.

The easiest way to conduct this comparison is to build an Excel spreadsheet that crunches the numbers for you. Since some readers might not have the skills to do that, I'm going to walk you through a step-by-step comparison to show how it is done.

First, we need to figure out how much money we will have after the sale of XXX and the funds we will have available after paying our taxes. Since XXX is now worth $70 a share on the market and we own 1,000 shares, we know that we will have $70,000 after selling XXX. Since this will be considered long-term ownership (because we owned the shares for longer than a year), we will now be taxed at 15% on the gains (in the future, capital gains tax will inevitable evolve from this number – be sure to do your homework and know the numbers as they change). The original price of the 1,000 shares was $50,000, so we can quickly see that we made $20,000 in the 3-year period. As a result, we will pay $3,000 in capital gains (found by taking 15% times $20,000) upon the sale of XXX, which means we will have $67,000 available to potentially purchase our new stock.

The capital gains calculation becomes very important

when conducting the comparison of two different assets. This calculation becomes exponentially important when the sale is done on a short-term basis (like day trading) because your capital gains are 30% or more – starting in 2013.

So the next part of the calculation begins with the purchase of company TTT with our $67,000. With that much money, we can purchase 1,340 shares of company TTT (remember it's trading for $50).

Now that we know how many shares we can own of the new company, we will simply conduct a time value of money on each asset to calculate the difference after a known period of time.

As we look at the growth of both assets, we'll assess their growth rate for the next 10 years based on the return we'll receive from the premium and discount we pay at the current market prices. Below is the calculation.

Start with this essential math equation:

$$FV = PV\,(1+i)^n$$

FV = The Future Value of Money (this is the estimated market price in 10 years)

PV = The Present Value of Money (this is the current market price)

i = The Growth Rate (This number is a little tricky to determine. You can calculate this number by using the www. BuffettsBooks.com intrinsic value calculator. Simply adjust the input for the 10 year federal note until the calculation equals approximately $70 for company XXX and $50 for TTT. Those numbers are the current market price for XXX and TTT. If you get confused, please look at the screen cutouts I've provided below.)

n = The Number of Years

In order to find i for company XXX, you'll use the following inputs on the intrinsic value calculator.

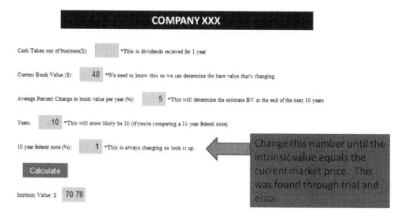

This calculation shows us that if we hold company XXX, it will continue to grow at 1% a year for the next 10 years.

In order to find i for company TTT, you'll use the following inputs on the intrinsic value calculator.

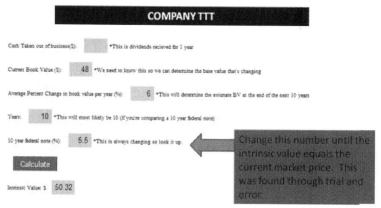

This calculation shows us that if we buy company TTT at the current market price of $50 a share, it will continue to grow at 5.5% a year for the next 10 years.

Now that we know the rate at which our two investments will continue to grow (1% for XXX and 5.5% for TTT) from the current market price, we can now estimate the value of the shares in ten years.

Here are the numbers for company XXX. You presently own 1,000 shares of this company.

$$FV = 70 * (1 + .01) \wedge 10$$

$$FV = \$77.32$$

This means that if you kept your 1,000 shares, in 10 years the value would be the following:

$$\$77,320 = \$77.32 * 1000 \text{ shares}$$

* * *

Now, let's do the same thing for company TTT. If you wanted to buy shares of this company, you could only buy 1,340 shares because of the capital gains.

Start with this essential math equation:

$$FV = PV (1+i)n$$

FV = The Future Value of Money (this is the estimated market price in 10 years)

PV = The Present Value of Money (this is the current market price)

i = The Growth Rate (found from above - 5.5%)

n = The Number of Years

$$FV = \$50 * (1 + .055) \wedge 10$$

FV = $85.41

This means that if you purchased 1,340 shares, in 10 years the value would be the following:

$114,449 = $85.41 * 1340 shares

As you look at the value only 10 years later, you quickly realize this decision to change your money into another asset is a $37,129 decision!

In fact, if you would compare the continued ownership of XXX to the 10 year federal note, you would find the note also provides a better return – even after paying the capital gains tax.

As you can see, the decision to switch assets shouldn't be guess work. To summarize, there are two reasons to sell your shares.

1. The company changes its fundamentals and it doesn't correspond with your values and direction. A great example of this is a change in leadership, increased debt loads, a substantial decrease in earnings capabilities, etc.

2. Mathematically, you have calculated that you can make more money in another asset with the same amount of risk after paying capital gains. Please note the term "same risk." That's an important part to consider.

I realize this chapter involves a lot of math. As a result, I've used this exact same scenario on the www.BuffettsBooks.com website. To watch the video that demonstrates this scenario navigate to course 3, unit 1.

Chapter 11
Understanding Return on Equity (ROE)

One of Warren Buffett's favorite terms to look at when purchasing a stock is "return on equity," or "ROE." In order to understand why this term is important, I'll once again use a scenario that most individuals can relate to.

Let's say we have a woman named Jill. She is a very successful woman who became a doctor and now makes a six-figure salary. Although she incurred a lot of loans and expenses, she's still able to save money every year. One day as she's reviewing her finances, she wonders if she'll ever become a millionaire. In an effort to see how much she's currently worth, she lists all her assets and liabilities (just like we did in chapter 7). After taking the difference between the two, she finds her current equity is $100,000. As she looks at how long it might take her to go from $100,000 to $1,000,000, she quickly realizes that the calculation is directly related to her net income (or the amount that's left over after she receives her salary and pays her bills). As she reviews her income, she finds that she made $120,000, but she also paid $100,000 in her annual expenses. This means that her net income was $20,000 – all of which was put into savings.

As Jill calculated how long it would take her to save up to $1,000,000, she quickly realized it wouldn't be fast. Without accounting for compound interest, she would only be able to save $100,000 every 5 years (assuming her net income never changed).

This comparison of current equity ($100,000) to her net income ($20,000) is a simple example of how businesses report their return on equity. For this scenario, the return on equity is 20% ($20,000 / $100,000). If Jill were a company, that would be an outstanding ROE! It's been my personal preference to invest in companies that consistently have an ROE over 7%.

The reason this number is so important is because equity

and intrinsic value are closely related. If equity goes up, the intrinsic value typically increases at the same rate and magnitude. If equity increases by 10%, then the stock value will typically increase by 10%.

Going back to the Jill scenario, let's really prove why ROE is important. Let's assume it's 45 years later and Jill made some really poor financial decisions. Although she's worth $1,000,000, she's still only earning a net income of $20,000. For the last 45 years, Jill took that same $20,000 and simply put the money in a zero-yield savings account. Since Jill never really invested her money in anything and she kept buying new houses and cars, she never increased her net income. Based on Jill's lackadaisical investing, let's calculate her ROE 45 years later.

ROE = Net Income / Equity

ROE = $20,000 / $1,000,000

ROE = 2%

Assuming Jill were a business, I think we can all agree that if we had to invest in Jill now, we wouldn't expect much of a return on our investment. Presently, she doesn't have the capacity to increase her net worth (or equity) faster than 2%, so if she were a business, that's all the more you could expect her value to increase.

As we examine the importance of the ROE from a perspective that makes sense, it becomes obvious why this is one of Warren Buffett's favorite statistics to examine. He knows that if he's buying a company that historically keeps a high ROE, that's going to be reflected in the market price over an extended period of time. When we looked at the Jill example, we could see that in the early part of her life, Jill had the ability to grow her worth (or equity) at a very substantial rate (20% a year). As time marched on, we found that Jill had no idea how to maintain that return on equity. If we were to understand why she didn't sustain her ROE, we could most likely attribute it to her inability to manage her debt and her ability to acquire more assets.

You might be thinking *How does this assessment of an individual relate to stock investing.* Well, I'd argue the parallel is almost identical. For many small businesses, they have a difficult time "breaking out" of their fundamental product. In some cases, you'll even see small businesses try to push a regional brand into a national market, and in the process, they incur large amounts of debt – which they struggle to repay. In the end, I often find small businesses start with a great ROE, but over time, it declines rapidly as they become a mid-cap and large-cap business.

(small-cap is when a company's market valuation is below 2 billion, a mid-cap is when a company's market valuation is between 2 and 10 billion, a large cap is when a company's market valuation is above 10 billion)

This is something really important to consider when buying your stocks. I personally like to purchase mid-cap and large-cap companies because they don't run as high of a risk for decreasing ROE. Essentially, I don't want to potentially invest in a Jill. Small caps might have a great ROE now, but how will they handle the transition when they need to do more than their current focus in order to sustain equity growth? Although I don't want to prevent you from investing in small-cap companies, I'd argue there's a lot less risk in maintaining your estimated growth with large ones. This approach is my personal attempt to never sell my shares. Remember, I don't want to pay taxes on a company that I might need to sell in 5 to 10 years.

* * *

When I analyze a company's value, I first examine the company's book value growth (which was taught in chapter 7), then I compare that figure to the average ROE. Typically, you should see similar numbers. If the book value growth is less than the ROE, I always try to understand why.

ROE = Net Income / Shareholders' Equity

Note: The net income is found on the income statement, and the shareholders' equity is found on the balance sheet.

If you would like to watch the video lesson that accompanies this chapter on www.BuffettsBooks.com, simply navigate to course 3, unit 2.

Chapter 12
Understanding Volume

W hen I ask young investors how the market price for a stock is determined, I often get blank stares. I think most people ultimately understand that the market price is determined by the price that buyers and sellers are willing to exchange assets for. Beyond that fundamental concept, things start to become foggy.

So let's dig a little deeper and really start to understand this exchange. Let's start with analyzing the stock price of a very popular American company – General Electric (GE).

At the time of writing this book, the market price for GE is $19 a share. So with that said, how many people determined that market price of $19? All the current owners? A few investment bankers?

Thinking about that question from an intuitive standpoint, some might think that the current market price is determined by all the current shareholders. If this is your initial thought, you'd be wrong. In fact, less than 1% of the owners generally determine the trading price.

Let's let the circle on the left represent the total number of shares of GE. As you can see, each little dot represents a share.

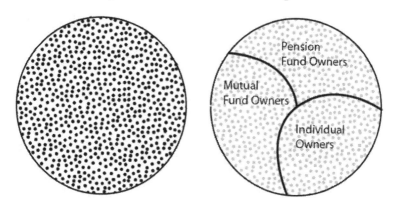

As you look at the picture on the right, you'll notice that I generically divided the total shares by three different types of owners. As you can imagine, some owners might own 10 shares while other owners might own 100,000 shares.

Now let's look at the people who are determining that market price. As you look at all the shares in the circle, almost none of the shares are changing owners from day to day. The number of buyers and sellers are actually a really small number compared to the total number of shareholders. The number of shares that change owners is called the volume. If we were to represent the number of buyers and sellers in a given day, it would look like the graph below. Remember, these are the very few people who are actually determining the market price of your company – not the value!

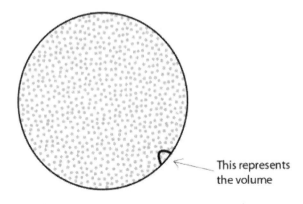

This represents the volume

When you take a step back and consider that such a small number of individuals are constantly determining the market price, you should quickly find comfort in knowing that the other 99% of owners may or may not agree with that market price. For example, during the time of writing, GE's volume was 44 million shares. This means 44 million shares were sold and bought in one day. That might sound like a large portion of the business, but when you check the number of shares outstanding, you'll find there are 10.5 billion shares. So when you divide the volume by the total shares, you'll see that only .4% of the owners determined the market price that day.

Let's look at this scenario in a more understandable system. Let's say there's a small business that's very successful in your town. Let's assume that 1,000 people in town each own 1 share of that business. As people in town become curious and try to determine the value of this really successful business, numerous different estimates are found throughout the village. As luck would have it, 4 people who hold a share of the business decide to sell their portion to 4 new investors. After the transaction takes place, many people in town are surprised to find that each share traded for $20. Most people actually thought each share was worth $35.

This little scenario is a great example of how investors need to always remain skeptical of any market price. To think that only 4 owners of the 1,000 would determine the total value of the business is actually amusing.

Now let's take this generic story to the next level. Let's assume that as time moves on, more and more shareholders sell their portion of the business each week. Because the market price was so low, many of the owners became a little worried and decided to get their money while they still could. Later in the month, the market price decreased further to $15 a share. As a result of the really low price, the volume of trades began to increase. In fact, 40 new people in the town were trading their shares every day. As the volume increased, the transactions were the talk of the town. It appeared there was a major argument among most people. In one camp, people felt the price would continue to drop; in the opposite camp, investors felt the market price was a total bargain and they bought the shares from the scared people.

In the following scenario, we could assume that the volume changed as follows:

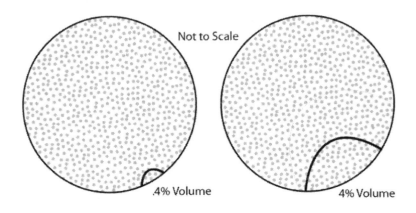

Not to Scale

.4% Volume   4% Volume

As you're beginning to think about how volume can provide you with useful information about the market price of your stocks, we can deduce the following:

An increase in volume means the traders believe there's a discrepancy between price and value.

Now whether they disagree with the price being too low or too high, that's for you to determine. But one thing is clear. When you see volume hit really high numbers, you can expect a peak or a valley on the market price. (I'm confident the methods you learned from Part II of this book will help you answer that important question.)

If you would like to watch the video lesson that accompanies this chapter on www.BuffettsBooks.com, simply navigate to course 3, unit 3.

Chapter 13
Mutual Funds Versus Index Funds

As you've probably discovered throughout this book, investing in individual companies or bonds isn't an easy process. If done strategically, patiently, and without emotion, you'll undoubtedly be successful. As I'm sure you might have deduced, investing in individual picks might be too confusing and difficult to enjoy. As a mathematical person, I love it. I've really tried to make sense of the intricate craft, but for some it may still seem like smoke and mirrors. As a result, you might have skipped a lot of chapters and immediately started to read this one.

Many people would much rather have someone else manage their money. As we've found, picking individual companies can be time consuming and frustrating if you don't like math. For many people who can't understand the intricate methods laid out in this book, they turn to "experts."

In order to have an "expert" invest their money, many people use mutual funds. As I'm sure you already know, a mutual fund is a financial organization that takes its shareholders' money and invests it in numerous businesses throughout a particular sector. Although mutual funds sound like a wise method for investing your money, many times they are not. In fact, Morningstar has determined that 70% of all active mutual funds will not even beat the market. Here's why.

1. Investors give fund managers money at the wrong time. Now that you've had some time to read this book and understand the importance of buying stocks during fear cycles and holding during greed cycles, this first indicator should make sense. To understand this principle, imagine that you're the fund manager of a $100 billion investment fund. When the stock market crashes and you're able to purchase severely un-

dervalued businesses with minimal debt, not only do you lack funds to invest, but all your resources are being depleted by scared investors. Instead of receiving money to buy the great deals, your investors are selling their shares in the fund and you don't have the capacity to take advantage of the market behavior. This reason alone severely handicaps fund managers as they attempt to beat the market.

Warren Buffett's primary reason for never running a mutual fund is based on the reason highlighted above. Buffett never wanted to be handicapped by uninformed investors. In a true display of his brilliance, Buffett actually found a way to take advantage of this phenomenon as opposed to being a victim of it. Instead of creating a mutual fund, Warren Buffett actually nested all his stock picks within his company, Berkshire Hathaway. This way, when people got scared and undersold the value of his business, Buffett simply purchased those shares of his company from the scared investors. Although Buffett's acquisition of Berkshire was somewhat of a blunder, his ability to turn the company into a shell for his investments is the important part to understand. Nesting his stock picks inside the corporation allowed him to take advantage of the fearful and ignore the greedy.

2. Fund managers suck the blood out of your investments with fees. For most mutual funds, you'll see fees range from 1% to 2.5%. Although this might not seem like much, let's put that number into perspective. Let's assume that we are working with an averaged-sized mutual fund of $5 billion and fees of 1.5%. Based on those figures, $75 million will be paid for the management of this fund. Now you might just chalk that enormous amount up to the cost of hiring a true professional, but I'd argue it's the price to flush the toilet – considering most funds don't outperform the market.

Let's see the impact of these fees over a long period of time. Assuming you invest $10,000 a year into a 1.5% fee-based mutual fund for 30 years, you could expect the following difference (assuming zero growth):

30 Year and No Fee	30 Year and a 1.5% Mutual Fund Fee
$300,000	$239,383

That's a $60,617 difference! Are you comfortable paying your financial advisor 20% of your initial investment? Essentially, that's what you're doing in this scenario. The numbers are pretty crazy when you look at it from this perspective. As you can see, the compound interest of your mutual fund fees will have a devastating impact on your investments.

3. Fund managers constantly move their assets to appease their owners. As we learned in Part II of this book, taking advantage of unrealized gains is one of the most important fundamentals for an investment to grow. For fund managers, lack of movement means they aren't doing anything. Since many mutual fund owners want a tangible reason to justify their 1.5% fee each year, they produce an "active" portfolio.

In order for this activity to occur, fund managers are constantly buying and selling assets. If you ask me, the buying and selling that is highlighted in each quarterly report is nothing more than propaganda for the manager's expertise – "expertise" you pay an enormous premium for every year.

* * *

Although I'm not fond of mutual funds, I highly encourage you to decide for yourself. If you're the type of investor who knows you're not going to purchase individual stocks and you find mutual funds a little fishy, then I'd like to focus your attention on index funds. Like mutual funds, index funds are also a conglomeration of different companies. The primary differences between the two instruments are a lack of fees, a lack of changing assets, and a lack of management. Now a lack of management might not sound like a good thing, but it actually is.

Have you ever wondered if you could simply invest in the S&P 500 or the companies that make up the Dow Jones? If you have, you already understand the concept of an index. An index is an unmanaged conglomeration of securities that represent a certain segment of the market.

For example, if you wanted to invest in an oil company, you could instead put your money in an oil index. Depending on which index you choose, you could invest in hundreds of the best oil companies around the world. The beauty of the index is that the fees are low (under .5%), and underperforming companies are automatically removed when competing businesses perform better.

One of the ways I've personally capitalized on index funds is by using them at the right time. Since different sectors of the stock market experience growth and recessions at different times, index funds offer a minimal amount of risk for entry into a depressed market. Due to diversification, index funds offer a safety net for investors in feared sectors. Although this is only one technique for investing in these instruments, you may even want to invest everything through indexes.

Since investing in index funds (or ETFs) isn't the focus of this book, I'm going to stop here. Regardless of your investment approach, I'm a huge supporter of index funds. I feel the minimal fees and proven track records make for better investments than mutual funds.

Chapter 14
The Wealth of Nations

As irony would have it, I experienced an interesting event at the dinner table the other night. As I began to bite into my wife's delicious meal, my 11-year-old niece asked me what the difference was between capitalism, socialism, and communism. As I chuckled, because I never thought I'd be asked such a complex question by an 11 year old, I asked where she had heard about those three terms.

"I learned about them in my social studies class. But I really didn't understand the difference," she stated.

As I prepared to respond, I could tell Jenny and her sister (Kelly, 14 years old) were already concerned about the length of my answer. For them, they often remembered how long I could draw out a response. Not surprisingly, my wife even started to snicker as I began to talk. (I get no respect, I tell ya.) Anyway, before I began with my definition of capitalism, I asked little Jenny if she had ever heard of a man named Adam Smith. To my surprise, she said, "Yes, we learned that he wrote a book called The Wealth of Nations. He was this guy who said the price of a thingee will change when people spend more money and stuff." Laughing hysterically, I commended my little niece. Unfortunately for her, I still began my long and boring dissertation on one of my favorite historical figures, Adam Smith.

Up until this point, I really haven't talked about Warren Buffett's third favorite book, An Inquiry into the Nature and Causes of The Wealth of Nations. Since the book you are reading is geared toward individual investing, I haven't found the right place to discuss Smith's famous macroeconomic principles. You might be wondering how I can possibly relate Smith's book to personal investing, but if you stay with me, you might find its importance paramount to everything else.

In 1723, Adam Smith was baptized in the country of

Scotland. Although his exact birthday isn't known, one thing many can agree on is that he changed the direction of the world forever. Many consider Adam Smith to be the founder of capitalism, but I'd argue he probably wouldn't appreciate that title. At the heart of everything Adam Smith represented were the ideas of morality and the focus on humanity. In fact, Smith's first book was titled The Theory of Moral Sentiments, and in his opinion, it was his magnum opus (or great work). During the time when Smith wrote this book, he was a teacher who specialized in moral philosophy. His primary goal was to explain the source of mankind's ability to form moral judgment. What he found was when individuals observe and understand not only themselves but others, they become aware of the morality of their own behavior.

As Smith became somewhat obsessive in his quest to enlighten and build a better world, he stumbled across an ironic circumstance – and it related to an individual's self-interest and economics. As Smith quickly discovered, individual greed and the motivation to earn money actually fuels a beautiful fire on a macro level. In Smith's book, he starts by identifying money as nothing more than work (or labor). As one can quickly understand, increasing the desire to produce more labor will result in more luxuries for all to enjoy. This monetary growth allows societies to grow and provide better facilities and services for its citizens. Smith's focus was not on creating material wealth for countries but creating a wealth of contentment for its citizens. As Smith studied "wealthy" societies, he learned they all had certain elements in common: citizens possessed individual liberties, limited government, open markets, and swift judicial systems. Like any focused genius, Smith took the next 10 years to focus on the open markets aspect in The Wealth of Nations. In the end, he produced one of the most comprehensive books ever written on macroeconomics. Many readers might view the purpose of his writing as a means to create a monetarily rich nation – and they would be 100% wrong. Smith's purpose in writing The Theory of Moral Sentiments, The Wealth of Nations, and his last and unfinished book, Jurisprudence, was nothing more than his attempt to create a better society for all to enjoy.

As I look at the purpose of this book, I can humbly say it's not nearly as noble as the reason for Adam Smith's books. With that said, I challenge all readers (including myself) to think about the purpose of Smith's vision. I have no doubt that if you adopt the principles outlined in this book and the ones they represent, you'll slowly become a successful and prominent investor. The important question to ask yourself is what do you do with it?

You might be a little confused as to why I put this chapter/ history lesson in this book, but for me, it's really important to ensure that our future wealthy citizens understand the purpose of their financial journey. Maybe for you, retiring with a monster house is important. I know I've dreamed of owning a beautiful sailboat someday. But when those difficult self-interest choices present themselves throughout our lives, I challenge everyone – including myself – to think about Adam Smith's life thesis: Have you empathized with the lives of others before making decisions that credit your own self-interests?

Common Stock Terms

Instead of describing where to find each ratio or term throughout this book, I figured it would be handier to have one location you can reference. Although I use Microsoft Money to show where I find all the different terms, feel free to use a program that's more preferable (i.e., Bloomberg). I've chosen Microsoft because it's a free program. In all the examples, you'll notice I use the stock ticker JNJ (Johnson & Johnson). This is simply to provide continuity from the lessons learned in this book. If you would like to watch a video where I demonstrate where each of the terms listed below can be found online, simply go to www.BuffettsBooks.com and select Course 3, Unit 4.

In order to get to the main screen on MSN where you'll enter your stock symbol, start at the following web address: http://money.msn.com/. From there, you'll enter the ticker you're interested in viewing.

* * *

Shares Outstanding: This is simply the total number of shares the business is broken down into. For example, JNJ is 2.73 billion shares. This is a really important number to know when you want to know what the total value of a business is being traded for. Since the current market price is $64.95 a share, we simply multiply the market price by the shares outstanding to get an idea of what the crazy traders think the value of the company is.

In this case, current market traders believe the value of JNJ is $177.3 billion. As you learned in Part II of this book, that's the market price, not the intrinsic value.

EPS: This means earnings per share. This number is the company's total earnings for the year divided by the number of shares outstanding. This number is really important because it tells you how much money your single share will make every year.

This number should be displayed on the first page you see after entering the ticker symbol you are researching.

The EPS is derived from the income statement. In order to calculate the number, you would go to the bottom of the income statement and take the net income divided by the shares outstanding.

EPS = Net Income / Shares Outstanding

To get an overview of the earnings forecast, locate the navigation bar on the left side of your screen and click on "Earnings." This will provide you with information on what professional analysts expect the company's earnings to be for the current and following year. You'll obviously want to see consistent or growing numbers.

P/E: This is everyone's favorite. It's commonly referred to as the "PE." This number is the company's current market price divided by the company's annual earnings per share (or EPS). Below is how you would calculate the P/E for JNJ.

The current market price is: $64.95
The current EPS is: $3.48

Therefore, the P/E is the following:

P/E = Price / EPS = $64.95 / 3.48 = 18.66

If you look on the top-level ticker page for MSN, it will automatically display the P/E ratio for you.

A great way to understand this ratio is to say the following phrase when you read it:

For every $18.66 (say the P/E ratio) I spend buying this company, I can expect $1.00 in earnings a year later.

Ensure you only replace the $18.66 when you read the sentence. The $1.00 in earnings never changes.

As a rule of thumb, Warren Buffett typically likes to find companies with a P/E lower than 15.

If you notice a statistic called the forward P/E, this number is calculated by taking the current market price and dividing it by the forecasted earnings for the next year. As one might expect, future earnings are very difficult to predict, and if the market price changes significantly, so does the forward P/E. I don't place much value in this statistic, but I do place a lot of value in the projected earnings for the following year. To view that forecast, click on the "Earnings" tab on the left-hand navigation bar.

Volume: This is the number of shares traded on any given day. The number is also reported on the top-level stock ticker page. For JNJ, on 15 February 2012, its volume was 2.3 million shares.

Remember, when the volume is really high, it typically means the market price is reaching a high or low.

Dividend Rate: This is the amount of money the company will currently pay you annually for owning one share of the business. For JNJ, the current yield is $2.28. Since most dividends are paid quarterly, this money will show up in your bank account every 3 months as $0.57 per share. This number can be found on the top-level stock ticker page.

Dividend Yield: This is simply the dividend rate divided by the current market price. Although this number is displayed on the top-level ticker page, it is calculated by the method below:

Yield = Current Dividend Rate / Current Market Price
3.51% =$2.28/$64.93

As you can see from the math equation, even if the dividend rate remains constant, the yield will change with the ever-changing market price.

As a rule of thumb, Warren Buffett always tries to buy companies that pay a dividend. I personally like to find anything with a dividend yield higher than 2.5%

Debt/Equity Ratio: This number is calculated by taking the company's total debt and dividing it by the total equity. Although you can conduct this calculation on your own from the balance sheet, you can find the ratio on the top-level information page after searching for your stock symbol. For JNJ, the debt/equity ratio is listed as NA. This simply means the number has not been calculated for you. As a result, we'll actually need to do it the old-fashioned way. In order to calculate the number, let's start with the formula:

Debt/Equity = Total Liabilities / Shareholders' Equity

Now, from the top-level stock page, look along the left side of the screen near the bottom where it says balance sheet. You'll want to click on that link. After clicking on the link, you'll see the page refresh with the information you need. In order to have the most current balance sheet, you'll want to ensure you've selected "interim" instead of "annual" at the very top of the sheet. As you look at the most recent quarter's report, you'll notice that all the values are reported in millions (this is fairly common for blue-chip companies). Since we'll be extracting both terms from the equation above from this sheet (and all the values are in millions), we won't need to add the zeros to the reported numbers. As you look at the sheet, you should be able to find the values from the equation above. At the time of writing, I'm getting my numbers from the third quarter of 2011.

Debt/Equity = $50,294 / $61,527 = .81

As a rule of thumb, Warren Buffett typically likes businesses to carry a debt/equity ratio lower than a .5.

Book Value (or Book Value/Share): This number is the equity divided by the number of shares outstanding. In order to find the book value number automatically calculated, you'll want to find a tab on the left side of your screen titled "Financial Highlights." After clicking on that tab, you'll notice the book value figure near the top of the screen.

In order to calculate the book value on your own, you need to go the company's balance sheet (found on the bottom left of the top-level page).

From there you'll want to use the following equation:

Book Value = Shareholders' Equity / Shares Outstanding

For the third quarter of 2011, JNJ had the following numbers:

Book Value = $61,527 / 2,732.25 = $22.52 a Share

This number is very important because it represents the value of the company if it closed its doors and stopped doing business. If an investor had the ability to buy all the shares and end the business, JNJ would be worth $22.52 a share. As we learned in Part II of this book, this number becomes really important as we assess a company's growth over an extended period of time. Warren Buffett and Benjamin Graham would often refer to this number as their margin of safety when comparing the premium they pay for a stock compared to its book value.

As a rule of thumb, a company's book value should increase by at least 7% every year. If the book value is growing at a rate lower than 7%, then the company should be compensating that growth with a larger than normal dividend. (i.e., above 2%). Please keep in mind this is a very general rule of thumb.

Price/Book Value (P/BV): This ratio is a way to determine the premium investors are willing to pay over the book value (or equity) of the business. To calculate the number, use the simple equation below:

P/BV = Current Market Price / Current Book Value

For JNJ, the P/BV is the following:

P/BV = $64.93 / $22.52 = 2.88

For you to understand what that ratio means, simply say the following phrase:

Currently, investors are willing to pay 2.88 (replace ratio here) times the BV (or equity) to own the company.

Many believe this ratio is very important because when you look at the P/BV over an extended period of time, you'll be able to see the premium that market traders have historically paid for the company. In order to see this running trend for JNJ, follow the guidance below to see the 10-year average.

From the top-level page, look on the left-side navigation bar and select "Key Ratios." After the page builds, look at the top left side of the nested page and you should see an option to select "10-YR Summary." After clicking on that link, you'll see a chart that summarizes the average for a few key figures. As you look at the top of the chart, you'll see the following:

	Price/Book
01/12	2.88
01/11	2.99
01/10	3.51
12/08	3.81
12/07	4.42
12/06	4.86
01/06	4.62
01/05	5.92
12/03	5.59
12/02	6.95

So as you look at those numbers, you can see that the premium investors have been willing to pay over the equity of the business has been consistently diminishing over the past decade. In order to understand that phenomenon, an investor would need to make sense of the numbers. In this case, I believe the market was absolutely overvaluing the company for the first 7 or so years. To pay a premium of almost 7 times higher than a company's equity usually never makes sense if you want to minimize your margin of safety. Substantially high P/BV ratios (anything over a 3.0) typically means unstable and unpredictable earnings – which breaks one of our essential rules.

As a simple rule of thumb, Warren Buffett typically looks for companies that possess a price/book ratio between .6 and 1.5. In order to purchase companies that have a higher P/BV, you'll want to ensure consistent earnings are expected in the future.

* * *

As a side note, when Warren Buffett was a young analyst and worked for Benjamin Graham, he wasn't afforded the luxury of using stock screeners in order to find potential picks. Instead, he would comb mammoth-sized books that listed stocks and their corresponding ratios. One of the methods he used in order to find potential picks was a simple math formula.

If the P/BV * P/E < 22.5 then it was a worth look.

When you break down the formula, you'll find that two of the rules of thumb I mentioned earlier produce the random 22.5 number.

When P/BV is 1.5 or less

And

P/E is 15 or less

You'll get the following result: 1.5 * 15 = 22.5

This was Buffett's very short way of comparing the market

price, to the equity, to the earnings, to the premium investors were willing to pay over equity, all in one.

To watch a video demonstration of this method, navigate to course 1, unit 1, lesson 5 on the www.BuffettsBooks.com website. Although this little formula is still pertinent, I recommend using the Google stock screener.

This wonderful tool allows you to add the exact criteria you are looking for. After you enter the information you want, you can then optimize the results so you can find businesses that really hit your sweet spot.

Equity Growth: This was one of the top things I discussed in the second part of this book. As I mentioned earlier, be careful that you don't review the equity growth from the balance sheet. Since the number of shares outstanding in a business change almost every quarter, simply looking at the equity on the balance sheet will not be a true indicator of the growth. The best way to review the growth is by analyzing the book value/share every year.

You can find this analysis on Microsoft money by following the same path as you did for the price/book ratio. Here are the directions again:

From the top-level page, look on the left-side navigation bar and select "Key Ratios." After the page builds, look at the top left side of the nested page and you should see an option to select "10-YR Summary." After clicking on that link, you'll see a chart that summarizes the average for a few key figures. You'll be looking for the section titled "Book Value/Share."

For JNJ, you should have the following figures:

	Book Value/Share
01/12	20.95
01/11	20.66
01/10	18.37
12/08	15.35
12/07	15.25
12/06	13.59
01/06	13.01
01/05	10.71
12/03	9.05
12/02	7.65

As you'll probably remember from Part II of this book, these numbers are a very large part of calculating a company's intrinsic value. Be sure to know exactly how to find these numbers. As mentioned earlier, you'll want to invest in companies that show consistent growth in book value.

As stated earlier, a company's book value should increase by at least 7% every year. If the book value is growing at a rate lower than 7%, then the company should be compensating that growth with a larger than normal dividend. (i.e., above 2%). Please keep in mind this is a very general rule of thumb.

ROE or Return on Equity: In the third part of this book, I devoted an entire chapter to understanding ROE. ROE was one of Warren Buffett's favorite numbers to look at. The easiest way to see the ROE for the past 10 years is to follow the instructions below.

From the top-level page, look on the left-side navigation bar and select "Key Ratios." After the page builds, look at the top left side of the nested page and you should see an option to select "10-YR Summary." After clicking on that link, you'll see a chart that summarizes the average for a few key figures. You'll be looking for the section titled "Return On Equity."

Many times, Microsoft may not have the most current ROE information posted on the portion of the site, so you'll want to follow the instruction below to find the current ROE.

From the top-level stock page, select "Financial Highlights" on the left-side navigation bar. After the page loads, you'll see the term "Return on Equity."

In order to manually calculate the ROE, look at the income statement and the balance sheet. Both of those pages can be pulled up from the top-level stock page on the bottom-left navigation bar.

The net income can be found near the bottom of the income statement, and the shareholders' equity can be found near the bottom of the balance sheet.

Here's the equation to calculate ROE:

ROE = Net Income / Shareholders' Equity

For JNJ, I calculated the following ROE for 2010. (Please note that I used the annual income statement and annual balance sheet.)

ROE = 13,334 / 56,579 = 23.6%

As a rule of thumb, you'll want to find a company that consistently has an ROE above 7-10%. This will allow the company to continue growing its equity at levels that will consistently put money in your pocket.

Current Ratio: I often use this ratio to determine the financial health of a company. If you remember the four tenants that must always be obeyed from Part II, chapter 7, of this book, you'll find the current ratio will help you with tenant 3: A stock must be managed by ethical and conservative (with respect to debt) leaders.

The current ratio is simply the current assets divided by the current liabilities. This ratio is important because it shows the potential investor if the company will need to incur debt within the next twelve months. According to accounting regulations, companies can only list assets and liabilities under the current section of the balance sheet if the money will be paid or received within a twelve-month period. As a result, this ratio gives potential investors great insight into the short-term outlook of the company. Below is the equation for the current ratio:

Current Ratio = Current Assets / Current Liabilities

In order to find these numbers, you'll want to find the company's balance sheet. The balance sheet can be found at the bottom of the left-hand navigation bar under "Balance Sheet." Once the page loads, be sure to find the location where the current assets and current liabilities are listed. Next, substitute the numbers into the equation above.

If you were looking at the numbers from the third quarter of 2011, you should have found the following numbers:

Current Ratio = $53,443 / $21,686 = 2.46

This is a great number. If the ratio was 1.0, then we would know the assets and liabilities are projected to equal each other. If the ratio was below 1.0, then the company would need to incur debt in order to continue business.

As a conservative investor, you want to ensure the current ratio is higher than a 1.5. This is typically the benchmark that Warren Buffett and Benjamin Graham liked to see in their investments.

* * *

As you look through all the different statistics and ratios, it might seem overwhelming at first. The only way you'll become comfortable learning these numbers is to look at companies that interest you, then start analyzing the numbers. As you can quickly see, familiarization with the balance sheet, income statement, and cash flow statement are vitally important. All the numbers being displayed come from those reports.

Although this recommendation might offend some readers, I'm going to suggest the book Reading Financial Reports for Dummies by Lita Epstein because it does such a wonderful job describing these corporate accounting sheets in an understandable fashion. Having read this book and Benjamin Graham's The Interpretation of Financial Statements, I can honestly say that the Dummies series does a better job at making the information understandable. If you're really considering adopting the principles found in this book, you'll definitely want to read more about corporate accounting.

Conclusion

Like I mentioned at the beginning of this book, the purpose of this project was to take three very complex books and make them understandable. Although some portions may not have accomplished that task for you, hopefully the key and important parts did.

Years ago I was just like you. I wanted to invest in the stock market because I knew there was money to be made. The only problem was I invested on emotion as opposed to value. In an effort to listen to my intuition, I went on a profound intellectual journey to definitively determine the methods of the world's greatest stock investor(s). In the end, I found these three books the centerpiece to Warren Buffett's investing secrets. He's a proven, intellectual success who uses a systematic method to invest. This book is my opinion of how it's done.

The key parts you've hopefully learned are the following:

1. There are four rules to investing. All four must be met in order to purchase an asset.
2. Financial markets move on emotion in the short term but follow value in the long term. As a result, always possess patience, knowledge, and think for yourself.
3. Every month you need to purchase assets in order to increase cash flow. Use that compounding cash flow to always reinvest in the most undervalued assets. In the end, it's all about share accumulation.
4. When you don't understand terms or concepts, do the research. That's the only way you'll ever know.

Remember, intelligent investors possess patience, knowledge, and discipline.

Recommended Readings

The Intelligent Investor, by Benjamin Graham

Security Analysis, by Benjamin Graham

An Inquiry into the Nature and Causes of the Wealth of Nations, by Adam Smith

The Interpretation of Financial Statements, by Benjamin Graham

The Bond Book, by Annette Thau

Reading Financial Reports for Dummies, by Lita Epstein

The Theory of Investment, by John Burr Williams

The Warren Buffett Way, by Robert Hagstrom

The Snowball, by Alice Schroeder

The Essays of Warren Buffett, by Warren Buffett and Lawrence Cunningham

Receive a
Free Signed Copy
of this book

I have created a Facebook fan page and a twitter account for Warren Buffett's Three Favorite Books. If you join either one of the pages, you'll be automatically entered into a drawing for a free signed copy of this book. The drawing will occur monthly, so don't miss out. In order to enter, simply Like the page on Facebook or follow us @BuffettsBooks on Twitter.

Thanks for your support!

Here are the links to both sites:

Facebook: https://www.facebook.com/BuffettsBooks

Twitter: https://twitter.com/#!/BuffettsBooks

About the Author

In 2010, Preston Pysh was the bestselling author of, *The Diary of a West Point Cadet*. His wide range of writing has been featured on a diverse host of networks like Comedy Central and the History Channel. He is a graduate of the United States Military Academy at West Point with a degree in aerospace engineering and has worked and  been deployed around the world. He's the founder of the Pylon Holding Company which is the parent organization of www.BuffettsBooks.com. His lessons on financial investing have been viewed and read by thousands of people all around the world.

Preston lives in Bel Air, Maryland, with his wonderful wife, Demi, their son, Tyler, and their two nieces, Kelly and Jenny. In his free time, Preston likes to read, play tennis, camp, and play golf.

For more information go to:
www.PrestonPysh.com

Or follow Preston on Twitter at:
@PrestonPysh

The Four Golden Rules

1. An investment must be managed by vigilant leaders.
2. An investment must have long-term prospects.
3. An investment must be stable and understandable.
4. An investment must be undervalued.

Notes

Notes

Notes

Notes

Notes

Notes

Made in the USA
San Bernardino, CA
24 June 2016